Road to the Unknown. The Nelson Mandela Path

SAMUEL O. BANAHENE

Cover design: Jasmine Correa and Author

The official release date of February 23rd, 2020, will mark my 10-year anniversary on American Soil.

Dedication

This Book is dedicated to my late father Kwasi Banahene, my lovely mother Mrs Grace Atakorah Banahene, the rest of my family members and to all the people that have helped me to reach this altitude in my life.

With Love and Gratitude

Special Tribute

2******************8****************24

Special tribute to Kobe Bryant, Gianni Bryant and the rest of the lives claimed during the 01/26/2020 helicopter crash in California.

I learned a lot from Kobe's mentality, which I continue to employ in my daily life.

May the souls of all the lives claimed in such a horrific tragedy rest in perfect peace.

Mamba Mentality For Life.

2

8　　　　　*Thank You Kobe*　　　　　*24*

2

Intentionally Left Blank

Table of Contents

WALKING THE WALK: LIFE AT SYRACUSE, UPSTATE NEW YORK

Nelson Mandela Quotes

❖ "A fundamental concern for others in our individual and community lives would go a long way in making the world the better place we so passionately dreamt of."

❖ "I learned that courage was not the absence of fear, but the triumph over it. The brave man is not he who does not feel afraid, but he who conquers that fear."

❖ "Everyone can rise above their circumstances and achieve success if they are dedicated to and passionate about what they do."

❖ "Education is the most powerful weapon which you can use to change the world."

Preface

They said I was not going to make it, so I chose the long road to prove them wrong. Life is beautiful, but sometimes we may find ourselves in the wrong place, one that can sabotage our goals if we do not block outside noise. Every success requires a journey to get there, and that journey is life. I defined life as turbulence flow. Depending on the task at hand, it may work as help or hindrance. I have been curious my whole life, and curiosity has helped me.

Growing up, I did not have anyone to serve as a role model. I used people's situations, both positive and negative, as ways to assess my own life. I quantified and characterized their circumstances to better myself moving forward. You may call it genius, but I defined it as wisdom. This philosophical approach led me to formulate three principles that helped me to reach my destination. I believe these three principles function together as a system, an architecture that will break down if one branch is omitted.

I do not define success as making millions or billions of dollars. Success is a person's ability to look back on his or her past and say with pride that, their circumstances never defeated him but rather made them stronger, compelling them to work harder to become the person they dreamt of being while growing up. Here are my three fundamental principles:

Firstly, BELIEF. You have to BELIEVE IN YOURSELF. This first principle was the foundation of my success. Every building has a solid foundation designed to hold it in place. This structural support allows the building to withstand catastrophic events such as the earthquakes imposed by Mother Nature. To achieve anything in life, you have to build that solid foundation to give you the confidence to set your journey in motion.

The second principle is HUMILITY. This is a critical part of my story because I was not the first person to take the road I took. You will need directions in order to continue on the correct path. The answers you get will depend on how humble you are. Keep in mind that when you humble yourself, you learn a lot because nobody wants to deal with an arrogant person. Your humility triggers the human desire to nurture and mentor the next generation. There are great people in this world who want to help you succeed. These people are not exclusively tied to your family, as you will learn from my journey. Therefore, be humble, ask for help, and you will get useful direction.

The final principle, which is the most important component of the system, is PATIENCE. In my eyes, this is where most people fail in their journey to success. They give up when things do not go as well as planned. I know that it is very difficult to deal with setbacks and disappointments but remain calm and wait for the right opportunity. Do not give up.

I hope my life story will give you hope and confidence to better yourself. For those who think they are worthless, poor, or have no role model, my message to you is stay positive; accept that everyone has moments of self-doubt and fear, but they will pass; and remember my three principles: Belief, Humility, and Patience. You will eventually get to the finish line.

Finally, do not forget to give back to your community once you get there. Aspire to inspire. Bring someone up too. By doing this, we all help to make the world a better place for everyone.

PART – I

CHAPTER 1

THE GENESIS: GROWING UP IN GHANA

i. Family

I was born in the Ashanti region of Ghana, West Africa, in 1992. I have four full siblings, of whom I am the eldest. The name of my hometown is Kona; with a population of less than 10,000. My mother had two sets of twins after giving birth to me. The first set of twins are two beautiful girls namely Mavis and Mabel. Followed by the second set, a beautiful girl Clementina and a handsome boy Clement. Our father was in the United States working as a taxi driver with only one properly functioning hand due to a stroke. My father married more than once; therefore, we do have half-siblings. Polygamy is common in most African countries, but my father did not practice it. All his marriages followed a divorce from the previous spouse, all Ghanaian women.

My mother was an elementary schoolteacher at an Islamic school located roughly fifteen miles from our hometown. We didn't grow up with our father. My mother said to me once that my father came to visit when she gave birth to me, but unfortunately, I was too young to remember him. The only way I knew him was through pictures that my mom showed us when I was about eight years old.

Cellphones were very limited at that time in my hometown. My mother did not have a personal cellphone, so our father used to call the cell number of a local extended family member who lived a few blocks away from us. He usually called on the weekends. For us to talk to him, the person with the cellphone had to be in town. I do recall having a conversation with him one time when I was ten. My first encounter with him happened when I was about twelve and he finally came to visit us in Ghana. I was very happy to see him but sad at the same time. Every child dreams of having both parents around when growing up. Well, that was not the case for us, but it was good to enjoy two months together in Ghana before he returned to the United States.

I grew up in a very large extended family. The beauty of it is that I got a chance to know my relatives. My mother's siblings gave birth to boys around the same time I was born. Therefore, I grew up with many male cousins in our family house. We fought all the time over alpha status in the home. The whole thing was like a lion king dynasty, where you get dethroned when you lose a fight. It was so much fun. There were about twelve cousins around the same age group in the family house. Among us, two were very brave or perhaps stubborn and didn't fear anything. Ezekiel was the oldest, followed by Lucky. I was the third oldest when accounting for the entire roster. We were all about a year and a few months apart. I do not know how that's possible, but it happened. The eldest one of us formed a soccer team, which consisted of the entire group of young lads.

We used to play soccer barefoot during the day with another local team. Ezekiel was a very good goalkeeper, and Lucky was a defender. My position was winger as a goal scorer. It was more like a local town soccer tournament. We were able to win many games during those tournaments. The games were played on the weekend, mainly Saturday afternoons and Sunday noon.

At night, especially when the full moon was shining, we played a game called hide and seek. During the nights when the moon was not out, we gathered around the fire and listened to folk tales such as *Kwaku Ananse Stories*, Akan folklore which originates from my tribe. Our Aunt Bofa was very good at telling these stories. Before we gathered around the fire, she would make sure each one of us had finished their house chores. At the end of each story, we would all get a chance to ask questions. I wouldn't trade my childhood with anyone; it was that good.

As most of you know, water is very scarce in most places in Africa. In Ghana, for example, we have two seasons every year, the dry season in the winter and the rainy season in the summer, dependent on the African monsoon. In the northern part of Ghana, the rainy season lasts from May to September. In the central part, it starts in April and ends in October. In the southern part, Ashanti Region, where my tribe is located, it starts in April and ends in November.

In my hometown of Kona, there was a water service that used to supply water to all areas with water faucets at a certain time, usually around noon, until the water tanks ran out. During the rainy season when it usually rained every three/four days, the plant was turned off because people would collect rainwater. The plant was finally shut down for political reasons, abandoning my town and limiting water resources. In the dry season, we used to walk more than one mile to fetch water. In most African countries, people walk more than six miles to fetch water; therefore, my two miles walking was a good deal! I remember my mother waking me up early around 3:00 am during the dry season to fetch water with my older family members.

My Aunt Mafia, who was the youngest among my mother's siblings, was the leader. She was a very brave and aggressive woman. In my tribe, younger ones are required to serve the older. It was a sign of respect. By waking up early, we were able to beat the line and get more water before it ran out. It was difficult sometimes, especially when the moon was not out. When it was dark, we carried lanterns.

I remember, sometimes, I would trip on something or step in a pothole and fall down due to the poor visibility. When such incidents happened and didn't crack my bucket and I was not far from the water, I would run back and fetch another. Even so, I was very scared to go by myself, thinking that something bad might happen to me.

Our neighbors used to wake up early as well; therefore, I usually saw people walking to fetch water. This reduced my nervousness, and I would say, "Thank God." We would roll together. Sometimes, if I was not lucky and tripped closer to home, which happened most of the time, I would just cry and go home with my aunt and the rest of the family members. It was very painful when such accidents happened because I always cut myself and started bleeding, either my toenail, elbows, or kneecap. It was tough, but that was what I had to do to support my mother and grandparents.

Two of my favorite grandparents were Nana Job and Nana Kwame. Nana Job's true name is Yaa Achiaa, but her church members called her Job, referring to the biblical figure, and that became her official name in our town. I wish I could explain why they called her that name, but I was too young to understand. "Yaa" is her traditional name, meaning she was born on Thursday. She was well respected in our town due to her generosity. She was a trader and traveled to the city to sell Kente, a popular cloth in the Ashanti tribe, during certain days of the month. Upon her return, she would buy bread, ice creams, fruits, etc. and distribute the bounty to all our family members and our neighbors. Her warm heart made her a unique individual in our family. I remember her mixing her dinner meal and dessert together before eating it. It was very gross to most of us, but she liked it that way.

One day, I asked her, "Nana, why do you usually mix your heavy meal and sweet stuffs together?"

She smiled and kindly replied, "Because that's how the food looks like in your tummy once you finished eating. I want to speed up the digestion process inside my belly." She was fun to have a conversation with.

Nana Kwame was the oldest grandparent in our family. His name, Kwame, originated from our tribe. It's a name given to males born on Saturday. He lived in Accra, the capital city of Ghana, and visited us every two months. I liked him because he knew all the family history. Any time he visited us, I was the one he usually sent to buy him small items such as bread, Lipton tea, milk, a razor, etc. I was very interested in learning more about my family history, and we would converse about those topics. Besides that, our Ashanti tribe is full of history, and we would talk about that as well. I acquired plenty of knowledge from him both historically and regarding general individual life. He was a very humble and quiet old man.

ii. Education system

In Ghana, the educational system is rigorous. All high school seniors in countries that are part of the West African Examinations Council, commonly known as WAEC, take the same standardized exams. These countries include Ghana, Gambia, Liberia, Nigeria, and Sierra Leone. This process makes the educational system highly competitive. I cannot speak a lot about my elementary years because I don't recall a lot! However, my middle and junior high school set the blueprint that would, later on, define the person I became.

iii. Middle and Junior High School

My middle and junior high school were combined. Thankfully, I lived three blocks away, which made my commuting distance less than others. Most students walked more than two miles to get to school every morning. If you were late, you would get beaten with a cane by the teachers. This practice—students beaten by teachers as a punishment—is very common in most African countries. Even though I lived closer to the school,

9

sometimes I was late. This was usually due to not getting up early to fetch water. I was tired, so I would sleep in a bit more.

I remember my friends coming in late and getting a couple of lashes before sitting. Most students would even choose to run away and not return for the day. Especially when the punishment was very severe. Sometimes, if the lashes were severe, I would have bruises on my ass; this made it very difficult to sit down and pay attention to what the teacher was lecturing about. I got very angry every time I was lashed. There was one girl who lived more than two miles from the school and therefore was late most of the time. She was beaten more often than anyone I could remember. I felt for her pain all the time and I wished our teacher had some sympathy for students who lived far away. This was usually not the case. It was very troubling, but what can we say; discipline was part of the educational system.

I grew up with a couple of bright, young people who realized that education was the key to success in this world. Growing up, we were taught about Nelson Mandela and what he was able to accomplish throughout the years by overcoming adversity. One of his favorite quotes that stayed with me is *"Education is the most powerful weapon which you can use to change the world."* There were four of us: Isaac, Prince, Emmanuel, and me. Among the four, three of us were neighbors: Prince, Emmanuel and me. English names were very common in Ghana since the country was colonized by the British and therefore most parents give their kids an English first name. Isaac, on the other hand, lived in a different neighborhood, which was a few blocks away from us. Even though my hometown was small, it still had different local names and so three of us lived in a neighborhood of one name while Isaac lived in different one.

We used to challenge each other throughout the school year to see who would come out on top. When school was over for the day, we would go home and do all our house-assigned duties such as fetching water, helping parents cook meals and other housekeeping activities. Later, at nighttime, we would gather in a house with light and do our homework. In my hometown, not every place had access to electricity. Sometimes, when the lights were out, which happened often, we would gather around lanterns and finish our homework.

One of my favorite teachers from middle school was Madam Doris. She was kind and inspirational. She was not fond of beating students with a cane. Instead, she would reward students who obeyed the rules with snacks and additional score points, which were added to your grade at the end of the school year. Madam is a very common honorific in Ghana, and we used it for all women teachers, but Doris was her actual name. During parent-teacher association meetings, she would talk to my friends and my mother to urge us to study hard. She made us believe that if we studied hard and followed our dreams, we would become successful. This mindset had a powerful influence on my life. My junior high school era, however, set the tone for my journey.

I started junior high when I was twelve years old. I knew the challenges that lay ahead if I failed to pass my final exam. Most people in my neighborhood failed to pass their junior high final exam and therefore were not able to get into senior high school. I saw how miserable life was for those folks. If I followed in their steps, it would be much harder, if not impossible, to achieve my goals in life. Because I wanted to go to college, I promised myself not to end up like that. At that time, I started to have conversations with my inner self about life, which is quite extraordinary for someone my age.

I initiated social experiments in which I observed and assessed individual lives based on the situation they were in and then used that to quantify and characterize my own life. I would project the likelihood of my future if I ended up in the same situation that another person was in, such as being involved with drugs, taking part in robberies, not taking school seriously and many more. You may call this "wisdom," but I define it as "determination" because I was not just chasing my dreams, I was willing to catch them. Because of individual life assessments that I made during my junior high school years, I decided to work extra hard and challenge myself on a completely new level.

During my first year in junior high school, I was assigned to a group. These groups were composed of members from all classes: first-year students, second-year students, and lastly senior-year students. The idea behind this was to create an energetic academic environment for all students. Group activities took place on Wednesday and Friday. For example, every Wednesday morning, we worshipped before classes; they preached to us about morals, kindness, and loving one another. After that, we would pray together, play drums, sing, and take a collection as you would at church.

This routine is common in most junior high schools in Ghana. The donations were not mandatory but rather given from the heart from each of us. At the end, the teachers would count the money and announce which group came out on top for that week. On occasional Fridays, we had physical education, such as playing soccer, running track, doing high jumps, and many other sports. The money collected during our midweek worship was used to buy sportswear and energy drinks for the participating members during these events. On other Fridays, we would have group quiz competitions. We competed in math, science, English, and sports.

I was chosen to represent my group during my junior and senior years. I was good at math, science, and sports, but English was not my strong subject. We came in first place twice and second place once. My teachers used to say I was a smart kid, but in my opinion, I was no better than the rest of the students; I just worked extra hard (this is called "humble" mindset because I refused to brag about myself).

I remember playing mind games with my friends, where we would notice how much time each of us was spending playing instead of studying. So, for example, when I saw someone that I was competing with playing, especially my three friends, I would pick up my book and go back to study. The idea was to be always on top of the heap. I utilized every opportunity to improve my

14

fundamental academic skillset over them. Because they may be smarter than I am, but they will never outwork me. Therefore, when they were playing too much, I was working, and that is called "the winning mindset" because I was hungry for success.

In the year 2007, my mother was finalizing her immigration paperwork to come to the United States. Let me tell you something about my mother. She is a very beautiful woman with a big smile. If we hadn't eaten, she would always make sure that our tummies were filled with food before she would serve herself. When my father's condition started to get worse in the United States, he couldn't send us money as he used to do. Things were very tough for us. The twins behind me moved to live with our grandfather and his wife. His wife's occupation was chef. The local town called her Original, meaning her food was authentic and delicious. Even though my mother was an elementary school teacher, her salary was very low.

In Ghana, the government employees are paid every month; this made it tougher for my mother to feed us, especially when they did not receive their monthly salary due to conflicts in the Parliament, in the country's capital, because of politician shenanigans. Therefore, my two siblings moving to live with our grandfather was a huge relief from stress for my mother. My siblings, Mavis and Mabel, assisted Original in the kitchen to prepare the food. My mother used to wake up early in the morning as well to provide some assistance to Original before getting ready for school.

I even cried most of the time because my mother was doing too much to support us by utilizing whatever was necessary to put food in our mouth. Through all, we stayed positive, knowing that, if I can focus on my education and work hard, someday I can help to revolutionize these circumstances. Her restaurant was open in the morning until noon and during the evening. Sometimes, it was even tougher for my sisters to get their homework done on time.

During my senior year in junior high school in March 2007, my mother got her visa to come to the United States to support my father. This was a huge relief for us because she would be able to take some stress off our father's shoulders and assist us financially back in Ghana.

In the same year, I was preparing for the biggest test of my life, which was the Basic Education Certificate Exam (BECE). In Ghana, during your senior year in junior high school, you select a couple of high schools you would like to attend in ascending order once you graduate junior high school. That is, ranging from your dream senior high school to the worst-case scenario. The subjects for the BECE include English Language, Ghanaian Language and Culture, Social Studies, Integrated Science, Agriculture Science, Mathematics, Basic Design and Technology, Religious and Moral Education and other optional languages such as French.

When my mother left us, we were living with our grandparents, so discipline was not always there. I had to push myself to study and prepare for that test. The house that we were living in with my mother did not have electricity. I used to study with a lantern. After my mother's departure, my remaining two siblings, Clement and Clementina, moved to our grandparents' house, so I had that room to myself to prepare for my final exam.

During the day, after school, I would go back to my grandparents' house, which was about two blocks away, do any assigned house duties as usual and then go back to school to study because it was a quiet place between 5 pm-6:30 pm. There was no security at the school after hours. All the necessary rooms were locked, but a few other ones were open.

In the nighttime around 11:00 pm, I would sit in front of my desk at home, put my feet in water so that I would not fall asleep, and study until 2 am. I did not have coffee to drink nor pills to take to help me stay awake. I did it all with passion and perseverance by believing that my future would be bright. I had faith and envisioned a better future. I took the BECE exam in June 2007 to finish my junior high school career. Our school district did not host any graduation ceremony for the senior students as most countries do.

After the test was over, I had to wait for two months for my results. During that summer, I learned how to weave Kente, which is a very well-respected and common cloth that the Ashanti tribe wear. While waiting for my results, I started making these Kente cloths and selling them for profit. Even though my mother was providing for us by sending us money during that time, I always wanted to do more on my own, to fight for myself, a confidence that I built along the way.

I saved all my Kente money and later on used it to buy some of my school supplies. Besides that, I farmed with my grandfather. He owned multiple fields in our town. They were all far away—at least ten miles. So during the days that I was not weaving the Kente, I would go to the farm with him. It was a long walk, so we would bring food and water with us. We had great conversations on our way to the farm.

I studied agriculture in junior high school and was able to utilize some of the skills that I gained in that course to assist my grandfather to increase the yield of the farm. We planted many foods, including maize, cassava, cocoa yam, yam, plantain and more. On our way back from the farm, I would carry some cultivated fresh food to bring home. We would put all the fresh food in sacks and tie them firmly; this made everything clump together so that I could carry it home on my head. Sometimes, it was heavy and we would rest at various places so I could catch my breath. There was one rest spot, next to a river, where all the other farmer would stop too. It was a perfect place to get fresh water and relax before continuing the journey. We usually stopped there on our way back home.

Our exam results came, and all my friends and I got into better schools. We were all happy but sad at the same time because that marked the end of our school time together. There were four of us, and we all got into different schools to pursue the careers of our dreams.

iv.   Senior High school

Senior high school in Ghana is similar to college/university in the United States. You can travel to a different part of the country for senior high school. Dormitories and meals were provided for those who were not commuting. I chose to commute by selecting a school closer to my hometown because my mother wanted me to stay near my siblings. I traveled about twenty miles every day to school in a passenger van. I attended Agona Seventh Day Adventist Senior High School in the Ashanti Region of Ghana. Something special about Ghana High Senior High School is that they offer various fields of study, and this prepares you for tertiary education.

My school offered courses such as accounting, science, home economics, general arts, and others. My first year, I started with business accounting; initially, that is what I decided to do. I was taking core class such as general mathematics, English, basic computer operations, and some other first-year classes. In Ghana, teachers rotate classes but not students.

One of my favorite teachers, JO, was my English teacher. I do not recall his full name! Every morning, he would give us some advice about life before diving into his lecture. He said something that stuck with me for the rest of my life. "It belongs to me and it belongs to us are two different things." He based his speech on a scenario of a rich family where both parents have resources to allocate for their kids when they die. He argued that tension might grow within the family about who should take the largest portion of the properties even though the parents may have an established will.

Therefore, he suggested, it's always better to fight and work for your own because that is the only way to truly put your hand on your chest and make the bold statement: "This is mine, not yours." I learned a lot from his speech because my father married more than once; therefore, I do have half-siblings. There would be opportunity for tension to grow regarding property allocation after his death. In order not to get into such arguments on who should have this and that, I decided to work hard. This would allow me to accommodate any financial needs my mother and full siblings might encounter if such incidents were to happen in the future.

During my first year, I fell in love with math and science, so I decided to switch courses. This was thanks to two of the amazing teachers who taught me these subjects. I changed from business accounting to science major in my second year. I was not behind in classes because in our first year, we were required to take the same subjects (*general cores classes*). That was a new challenge for me, but I was prepared for it. We had many smart students in the class competing for a top ten spot out of a class of roughly fifty students. I was constantly on my toes studying because I kept telling myself "winners don't sleep." This attitude was not new to me. It was just a new phase in my life, and I was standing tall and ready for it. Senior high school lifestyle in Ghana is similar to college life in the United States. I have categorized it into three sections: "The Observers, The Participants, and The Conqueror/Takeovers."

So, knowing that there was a goal that I wanted to accomplish in my life, I decided to hang out with people on a similar wavelength because when you associate yourself with such people, it challenges you in every way and brings out the best in you. In order to achieve your goals in life, you need to have positive energy. One of my best friends, Forbi, was a very smart person, and we used to compete against each other all the time. I met Forbi when I transferred to my new major. He was a commuter as well and lived in town, which was closer to my town, Kona. He was a big guy, very humble and intelligent. His career aspiration was to become a doctor and save lives. He helped me many times with homework that I was struggling with and vice versa.

During that period, my parents were working on immigration papers for me to come to the United States.

In Ghana, most people whose parents are financially stable and travel abroad for business-related activities usually don't study hard. They think that their parents are financially stable enough that they do not have to challenge themselves in schools. This is not true for all of them; some do work hard as hell to replicate their family's success and uphold their standards or reputation. Some will graduate with mediocre grades and still get into university because money speaks, and that sums up the corruption in Ghana's educational system. Others may not even finish, and that is just the way it is, unfortunately. For me, that was not the case. I kept Mr. JO's statement with me and wanted to work even harder and fight for my own.

In my senior year (4th year) in 2010, all my immigration papers were ready. It was time to part ways with my friends. I was very excited and sad at the same time. It is not always easy to leave those that you grew up with, but as they say, it's part of life that we must sometimes endure, part of growing. I told Forbi that I was going to the United States and that this would be the end of our friendship for the moment. He was very happy for me and emotional as well. I knew that he would do great in life because of his work ethic.

On the family side, I was sad to leave my siblings behind, but I knew that they would soon join me. Prior to my departure, I always thought of the United States as paradise. A place where your dreams can become a reality. Plenty of universities to enroll in after you have completed high school to pursue a career in a field of your interest. A place with advanced technologies to transform our world. A peaceful nation with fewer crimes due to U.S. military involvement with multiple countries to maintain peace. Zero hunger, no homeless, no poverty, and everyone enjoying life to the fullest. That's what I saw on TV in Ghana. I was very excited to experience such a luxurious lifestyle. I departed Ghana in February 2010 to come to the United States.

PART – II

CHAPTER 2

BEGINNING OF THE END: COMING TO AMERICA

Two days before my departure, my family member, Auntie Grace, assisted me throughout the immigration process before I was issued a visa and I left Kumasi, Ashanti region, to travel to the capital city of Ghana, Accra, where I would take my flight from Kotoka International Airport. Auntie Grace is a very nice woman with a big heart. She lives in Kumasi, which is one of the biggest cities in Ghana. She played an integral part in my immigration paperwork. She knew the capital city of Ghana, Accra, much better than I did because she used to work there. She always made sure that I was comfortable during our travels.

I remember for a United States embassy appointment, we would travel to Accra from Kumasi a day before the appointment and stay in a hotel. Once the appointment was over and we had time to spare, we would tour the city together, going to historical places such as The Independent Square also known as The Black Star Square. This site host Ghana's Independence Day parade every 6th of March to pay tribute to the bravely men and women who fought the British colonists and sacrifice their lives for the country's freedom. It was so much fun! So during the last two days before my departure, we took public transportation, one of these coach buses. It was roughly 260 kilometers. During the ride, I remember telling myself about the opportunities that awaited when I got to America, such as access to a high-level education. I was very excited, and I thanked God for this amazing opportunity, but at the same time, I was nervous. Leaving my family and the people that I grew up with was not easy. That day was very emotional.

The third day before traveling to Kumasi from my local town to Auntie Grace's house was an emotional one. In Ghana, during these travels, it was suggested to keep your mouth shut and not spread the word about such a journey due to some superstitious belief that someone jealous may harm you. Because of this, only a few people in my local town knew about it that, I was leaving. My last siblings, the second set of twins (Clement and Clementina), didn't even know that I was traveling to Mom and Dad, though in their case it was because they were too young, about seven years of age. Telling them would have elicited an intense emotional response, which would have been difficult for me to handle. They always looked up to me as their senior brother who protected them. To tell them I was leaving them would cause a humongous worry and sadness. They turn to be very emotional and cries a lot when something doesn't sit well with them and even refused to eat at times. Therefore, to avoid such an incident it was better for us all not to tell them about my travel.

A few extended family members in my town knew about my travels. The day before travelling to Kumasi to meet Auntie Grace, some of these family members gave me a woven Kente to present it to my mother when I got to the States—a sign of love in our tradition. Others asked me to give their warm greetings to my mother as well. They were all sad and happy for me at the same time. Before departing, I promised my sisters (the twins behind me) that I would do whatever it takes to assist my mother so that one day they could also come to the United States because they knew about our father's conditions as well. I saw tears coming out of their eyes. I remember telling them to be brave and take care of the younger ones.

The day of my departure arrived, and it was finally time to say my last goodbye to Auntie Grace. She told me to stay positive and keep my head up when I got to America so that I could eventually support my mom in bringing my remaining siblings to the United States. I accepted her advice with love and promised her that I would do it. She looked back at me, smiled and said you will do great. I passed through all the security checkpoints and was waiting to board my flight. I was looking around and seeing families traveling together in contrast to my lonely travel. I was seventeen and had never been in a situation like this. It felt uncomfortable. I didn't know anyone on that flight to talk to. It was a long flight, twelve hours, and the worst part was that my stomach was not being kind for this first flight of my life, but I made it through.

Once the aircraft took off and we started cruising, I asked myself: how is this thing flying? This small piece of metal is floating in the air about eleven thousand meters above the ground. When processing that thought, part of me said anything is possible in America. I knew airplanes were invented in America, as well as of other things important in the modern era. I knew education was the key to success, and I believed I could become somebody if I followed my dreams—and got an American education.

In the science field, our teachers told us that in America, there were many resources to support students to understand theories better through experimentations. In my science classes in Ghana, I learned about scientific theories and how systems function. However, limited experimental resources made it harder to quantify some of these theories or to experience them firsthand. This was a huge drawback to us and knowing this would change when I got to America was a great feeling.

We finally made it to JFK International Airport. Once the aircraft touched down, everyone started clapping and cheering the pilot for such a successful flight. I did too. I exited the plane and then started to panic. How was I going to find my parents? I went through the new arrival section to get my fingerprints recorded by Homeland Security and then handed in the supporting documents to be registered in the system. Everything went successfully, which I was glad of, but then the panic attack kicked in again. Where was I going to find my parents? I was a poor lad lost in the crowd. Prior to my departure from Ghana, my mom said they would hold a sign with my name written on it, but that did not help. I got out and saw many people waiting for their family members and friends. It felt like the Eddie Murphy movie, *Coming to America*. I started looking around to see if I could spot my mother.

Because I had not seen her in three years, it was even harder to spot her in the crowd. But as they say…"every mother knows her kids." My mom spotted me and called my native name "Kwabena," which means I was born on Tuesday in my Ashanti tribe. She used to call me by that name all the time when she was in Ghana with us. As soon as I saw her, I ran to hug her, and she was very happy to see me. She was there with one of my family members to pick me up I landed at eight pm. After going through the new arrival process, I left with my family around 10:00 pm. It was very cold compared to our tropical weather in Ghana, but it was a great feeling to come to America. When we left the airport, I started looking around and realized that infrastructure was well advanced, with multiple bridges and tall buildings. It looked like the America I had heard of growing up in Ghana.

When we got home to Mount Vernon, New York, I saw my father for the first time in five years. It was a very emotional night for me. We had not lived together for more than three months my whole life prior to my arrival. I wanted to hug him, but his condition did not allow me to do that. My father had been battling a stroke and diabetes for a long time. When I got home, he was lying on his bed and gave me a handshake as a welcome. It was late at night, so I left him to sleep.

My parents had a one-bedroom apartment, so I crashed in the living room, which was going to be my sleeping place for the next two and a half years. I did not complain about sleeping in the living room. I had seen worse in Ghana, so it was fine with me. My father was a disabled person, so he had a home care aide who came every day to take care of him, my mother informed me that night. She told me to wake up early and put my sleeping blankets and pillows away before the aide arrived at 8:00 am.

My mother's occupation is homecare aide as well, so she would travel to other patients' houses to assist with their need. I was in disbelief that the government was providing such an assistant for senior citizens. I asked my mother why she was leaving the house to perform similar responsibilities somewhere else when she could just take care of my father and get paid for it. She replied with a smile, saying that's not how things work in America.

In addition to this, she worked for a different agency, which was not responsible for assisting my father with his needs. It felt strange to me, but I was eager to learn more about my new environment and its culture. So when my mom came back from work around 6 pm, she would prepare dinner for us. My father's home care aide leaves around 4 pm. I felt for my mom because in my eyes, she was doing too much. Remembering how she was sending us money every month back in Ghana, I couldn't have been prouder of how she kept on doing so, given her circumstances. In gratitude and with respect for her hard work, I helped her with housework and dinner preparation.

CHAPTER 3

THE BLUEPRINT BY MY FATHER

Seeing my father's condition every day was tough to handle. Due to the stroke, sometimes he would go off and insult me, even though I had done nothing; it was difficult to handle at some points. Sometimes it felt like he was not my biological father. The stresses were tough when his temper was high. He even forgot who he was when this happened. I got very angry at times and would have to go for a walk to calm down before returning to the house. Nevertheless, I understood his condition, so when he got mad and started insulting me, I accepted it with a generous heart and calmed him down. I came to the United States because of him; he initiated my paperwork before my mother joined him in the States. In every situation, I always look at the bigger picture. In this case, it was that he gave me a chance to start a new life.

Two days after my arrival, we went to the Social Security office to get my Social Security card so that I could start high school. Our apartment did not have an elevator, and we lived on the third floor, so it was difficult for my father to get out of the house. It took him up to thirty minutes to get down to the first floor. There were six different stairways to get to the first floor with two landing platforms in between. He would take a break when he reached the platforms to catch his breath before continuing. My parents could not afford a place with an elevator. My father had a caseworker but unfortunately, she could not find an apartment on the first floor within the budget for my parents. My father received a Social Security benefit for rent, but it was not enough to cover the full payment; therefore, my mother contributed.

As a young man, I looked at this condition and I asked myself, "What can I do to support my family financially?" We still had four siblings back in Ghana that my mother was feeding, and if I included the extended family, then it was a completely new level of struggle. I thought I was escaping poverty by leaving Ghana, but instead, I inherited a different kind of poverty in a different world. I watched my mother leave the house every day around 6:00 am to take public transportation to get to work on time. Depending on the case she was on, she might travel to Yonkers, New Rochelle, different part of the Bronx and sometimes even Manhattan. When there were no cases available, she would stay home unpaid, and that was hard to watch sometimes.

After we applied for Social Security about two weeks later, I got my card. The next step was to start high school. With the help of the aide taking care of my father, we went to Mount Vernon Board of Education for high school placement. Prior to my arrival in the States, I got a transcript from my high school in Ghana because I wanted to continue my education. We completed some papers at the Board of Education, and they made a copy of my transcript. The Board assigned me to Mount Vernon High School.

The next day, we went to Mount Vernon High to complete the remaining process. It was a very different environment than Ghana. As an incoming immigrant, I was informed by the physician at the high school to complete some vaccines in addition to those I had gotten in Ghana. The United State embassy requires that any incoming immigrant complete a certain schedule of vaccines.

The school physician gave us a form to take to the nearest hospital. Mount Vernon Neighborhood Hospital was the closest to our apartment, about five blocks from us. My father was worried because I did not have any health insurance. We went to the hospital the next day with the help of his homecare aide. When we arrived at the hospital, we explained the situation to the registrar at the front desk. They told us to bring my mother because she was the one who was working and she could add me to her insurance. Without the insurance, they could not allow me to see a doctor.

My father was very sad and also tired due to his condition. He sat down on a chair to recover his breath before we headed home. While he was resting, a man named Dr. Mensah saw my father from a distance and came to us. Dr. Mensah was part of the upper-level management at Mount Vernon Neighborhood Hospital. He had been there for many years, and his words carried weight. He started by saying...I remember you from a couple of years back in the early 2000s. You used to give me a ride to work all the time. My father had been a taxi driver in New York City, using his own car. During the early stages of his stroke, he was able to drive. That was his primary source of income and how he supported us financially.

Dr. Mensah was Ghanaian as well and one thing about Africans is that, once in the United States, we love and appreciate each other even back in the motherland. Dr. Mensah continued to say that he used to call my dad to pick him up and drop him off after work. He appreciated my father's kindness and the love that he showed during that time. He asked us what we were doing here. My father explained the situation, and he offered to help us. He took us upstairs to the second floor, the adolescent medicine department to meet a physician's assistant named Dr. Lee Barry.

As a young lad who liked to observe and learn from situations to assess my own life, I learned a lot from what happened at that moment. In life, you never know whom you may come across again, so extend your hand and love to others. Dr. Barry had been practicing medicine for many years. He had been with the department for a very long time per our introductory conversation. Dr. Barry was very kind to us and extended his hand to help us. I was able to get the vaccines required, and he signed the form to return to the school physician in a sealed envelope.

Because of this, I was able to start school. The vaccines were a few weeks apart, but I was able to come back and complete the rest.

During that process, I started to build a strong relationship with him. He told me that he was from Africa too, but he never told me which part. Dr. Barry realized how humble I was, and he decided to give me advice about taking care of myself and staying off the street. I remember saying to him...education is the key to success and he kindly replied to me...you're damn right, Sam. Getting advice from someone at that high level felt amazing, especially not having any role models of that caliber.

I started high school toward the end of the third marking period in April 2010. The Sunday before my first Monday in high school, my father sat me down and gave me "The Blueprint." He said to me, be careful not to associate with any bad group because there were plenty of them here in America. He continued: Look at my current situation; I don't have the money to support you now, so make sure to find a part-time job to support yourself and your mother if you can...always remember where you come from and make sure to work hard.

I took what he said to heart. I knew he was speaking the truth. I had already established a hard-working attitude in

Ghana, where I used to put my feet in water to prevent me from falling asleep while studying. The mentality was not to go to sleep when I was tired but when the work was finished. Back in Ghana, sometimes, I would go to sleep early and wake around 3:00 am to study because by then everything was quiet, and that helped me to focus and get my work done. So in the United States, I knew that education was a critical component of my life as I looked to the future.

To me, education was the weapon to protect my family and me; therefore, I was willing to do whatever I had to sacrifice to go to college. Because of this mindset, I was standing tall and ready to start high school in America. I knew that this was going to be a new challenge in my life, but I was ready because I believed that I could do it.

CHAPTER 4

LIVING IN MOUNT VERNON, NY

M ount Vernon is a small city north of the Bronx, New York. It is part of Westchester County. This city was a second home to my father as he always described it. It was a new environment for me. I didn't understand the lifestyle, culture, or slang. My block was within walking distance to grocery stores and clothes stores. Every day was a new experience, as I needed to adapt quickly. To my advantage I knew how to speak English. A bit of history: Ghana was colonized by the British as I have stated previously; therefore, the English language became part of the basket of eleven languages spoken in the country. English became the common language among the different tribes. I had been learning and speaking English since kindergarten. My accent was very thick, though, and at first, this made it difficult to communicate with people. I would have to repeat myself multiple times for them to understand what I was saying.

i.   High School: 10th Grade

My first day at Mount Vernon High School as an incoming student was exciting and nerve-racking at the same time. What surprised me the most was the security. Students passed through metal detectors, were patted down and their backpacks were scanned to make sure that nothing illegal such as firearms, knives and other contraband, were brought to school. I was very confused as to why they were doing this. I asked one of the security personnel, and she explained it to me.

We did not have metal detectors in Ghanaian schools. There was not a lot of security, and no students ever brought such things to school. The moral standard was very different compared to my new culture. This incident made me wonder whether there's any discipline in American Schools. After going through the security checkpoint, I met with my assigned counselor. I wish I could mention her name but unfortunately, I cannot due to what happened later. She went over my high school transcript from Ghana and decided to assign me certain classes. I started school toward the end of the third marking period. I was in a weird position in terms of grades. I was more like a tenth or eleventh grader and because of this, it was a little harder for her to place me into the right classes. I was placed in Algebra, Global History 1, Earth Science, ESL, and some other classes. I recalled her saying she wanted to place me in the hardest math class at my level; therefore, I was given algebra. After our meeting, I navigated my way to my first class, which was algebra. The school was huge compared to what I had seen in Ghana. In Ghana, teachers rotate sessions, not students, which was the opposite of the United States.

I was very scared when I entered the class. Everyone was looking at me and wondering who this kid is. They were in the middle of taking a test. I spoke to the teacher—her name was Ms. Rosegue—and told her that I was new here. Ms. Rosegue was a very nice Caucasian woman, always with a big smile. She gave me the test and said just try it. I sat down, looked at the questions and smiled. Within a few minutes, I returned the paper to her. She was very surprised; she quickly graded my work while the rest of the students were still solving the problems. I got everything right.

After class, she told me that I was in the wrong class because I know this level of math already. The next day she gave me a New York State Regents exam to take; I passed it. "I will talk to your counselor so that we can place you in Geometry," she said. I went to my remaining classes. The following day, Ms. Rosegue said to me that my counselor was refusing to place me in Geometry. She decided to talk to her other colleague, Ms. Robins, who taught geometry. Ms. Robins decided to allow me to audit her class. Thankfully, both classes were offered at the same period, so every day, I went to the geometry class instead of algebra.

About two weeks into classes, I received a notice from my counselor to take Global History 2 instead. I didn't bother to argue because I was afraid. It did not bother me that much because I was determined to succeed, and nothing would derail me from achieving my goals. About four weeks later, I was informed about the New York State Regents, which was given at the end of each school year. I had to study extra hard to catch up on all topics, especially having been placed in Global History 2 in the 4th marking period. The test time arrived, and I was able to pass all the classes, including the audited geometry. Ms. Rosegue allowed to me take the algebra Regents, even though I did not go the class. I passed that as well. Taking algebra Regents, as suggested by Ms. Rosegue, helped to eliminate any potential issue that may have arisen with my counselor.

It was very tough for me to make friends in this session. During lunch periods, I would walk to the cafeteria and sit by myself. The food they served was different from what I used to eat back in Ghana. So, sometimes I would throw it in the trashcan, drink the milk and eat some fruits. I informed my mom about this, and she said it was normal and it would take time to adjust to their food. She had encountered the same problem, as it was tough for her to buy certain meals at fast-food restaurants. After she heard my situation, she started making me sandwiches to take to school for lunch. It felt like real food.

ii.   Summer 2010

That season was a big hustle. After school ended, I thought it was time for me to rest after working extra hard to pass the New State Regents. Instead, my father started yelling at me to get out of the house and find a job. Due to his condition, sometimes he would just go off for no reason. With all these insults, I took everything that he had

45

to say to heart because he wanted the best for me—to be a man. In my culture, especially when you are the oldest among your siblings, the parents demand you do more to support the family. Since I was the oldest, he insisted I stand up, stay hungry and get out of the house to find a job. He referenced my mother's current job, his own condition, and my four siblings in Ghana to encourage me to find a job. I had recently turned eighteen, was new to this country and didn't know where to look for work, but I took the challenge. I didn't have any money for transportation for summer job hunting. I used to walk to New Rochelle from my place in Mount Vernon, which was about four miles in each direction, to search for a job.

I applied to all kinds of fast-food chains such as McDonald's, Wendy's, Golden Castle, etc. and companies like Staples, Target, Best Buy, clothing stores—anything that could help me make some money to support myself and my mother. I did the same thing in Yonkers, which is roughly seven miles from my house. I remember that summer was very hot, and it was tough walking under the scorching sun looking for a job. As a boy, this struggle did not bother me that much because in every situation, I always looked on the bright side. Therefore, I took this opportunity to understand what life is about—hard work, go get it, or it will never happen. After a long search, about three weeks into the summer, I was able to find a job at a small fast-food restaurant, Chicken Hut, on 3rd avenue in Mount Vernon. It was within one mile from my house, so I was very happy.

My primary role was to be in the kitchen coating chickens with flour before frying, cleaning utensils, mopping the floor, and finally keeping the customer area clean as well. It was a lot of work and very stressful. I was getting paid $7.00 per hour, and sometimes, I was even sent home when business was slow. I did not have a cellphone, so communication was tough as well. We had a landline at home, and that became my primary point of contact, assuming I was home when a call for me came.

Three weeks into my job, I was ready to find something else. In Ghana, I was learning how to weave a Kente. I had a boss who trained me to become proficient. It was not stressful at all compared to what I had to deal with at Chicken Hut. I did understand the demands of the employees working at this restaurant, but it was just too much for me to handle.

There was a sneakers and clothing store named VIM on 4th avenue in Mount Vernon where I had to applied for a job earlier. The manager was very kind; his name was

Amaudo, and he was from Burkina Faso in West Africa. I told him I was from Ghana. Just a bit of geography: Ghana and Burkina Faso are neighboring countries. The two share borders and he had been to Ghana multiple times. Amaudo told me to come back during the "back to school" period (September), and he would hire me because at that time business would pick up.

In September I went back to him and requested an application for employment. I received a call from him about a week later to come and complete the hiring process. Once I completed all the paperwork, I told my manager I was leaving for another job. I was very happy about this new opportunity because it was less stressful than my previous job. My role was to assist customers in the sneaker department, answer calls, and do inventory; my pay was $7.50 per hour. It was a good job and I used to work forty-hour weeks and sometimes even overtime. I was paid every week, so I opened a bank account to save my money for college.

Finally, I purchased my first phone, Boost Mobile, which made communication much easier going forward. Due to my performance during the back-to-school period, Amaudo decided to keep me on the job part-time when high school started again. Amaudo and I had a great relationship. He was a very humble man and wanted his employees to feel comfortable doing their job. Amaudo's favorite sport was soccer, a very common sport across the African continent. I love soccer as well. We used to talk about European tournaments, such as the English Premier League, Spanish La Liga, German Bundesliga, Italian Serie A, and others all the time. It was so much fun because having a manager who shares similar sports interests as you is rare.

iii.   11th Grade: Junior Year

My father was very happy that I got a job. Being able to ease some financial stress off my mother's shoulders was a great feeling. Even though my father was excited about this opportunity, however, his anger issue didn't fully disappear. As time passed, I contemplated how to deal with him in a peaceful way. My summer job helped me to buy all my school supplies for the upcoming academic year. This academic year was my full start at the high school, so I was very excited and ready for the challenge. I enrolled in Physics, Trigonometry, Spanish I, English, US History, Arts, and Physical Education if I remember correctly. That year was very important for me because it was time for me to learn American history. I got the opportunity to learn about my history back in Ghana through both at school and from my grandparents. I understood how humans in Africa were traded and learned about the wars before Ghana finally gained its independence. Now, it was time to learn what happened next, when Africans were brought to America.

I had an amazing teacher named Ms. Linda. She was Italian, very lovely and kind. I really enjoyed her class as well as the rest. Ms. Linda helped me to understand American history—the good and the ugly. I recalled my math class, my teacher, Mr. Ratnathicam, a very smart man, used to ask general questions to the class. I would raise my hand and answer, but because my accent was so thick, it was hard for the rest of the students to understand. Mr. Ratnathicam, whose roots were in Sri Lanka, had to rephrase my answer for the class.

As time went on, my accent started to get better and communication became a bit easier. In terms of making friends, though, not a whole lot. I sometimes missed my friends from Ghana, wishing they could be here with me. It felt like trying to fetch water with a fishing net. I had to change the net to a bucket, or I would forever be without water! Therefore, I had to get out of my comfort zone to meet people.

During my first year at the school, I met a person name Yaw from Ghana. He was in his last year at the school and used to show me around sometimes during our lunch period. Unfortunately, he was not around anymore during my 11th grade, and I had to make new friends.

I met a couple of people from Haiti, Jamaica, and part of my own continent's Ivory Coast. It all happened at the cafeteria, the dining table I always sat at during the lunch period. We all had the same lunch period, so they saw that I was always quiet and started talking to me. They asked where I come from, and I replied Ghana. They introduced themselves as well.

As time progressed, we all became close friends. We used to walk home together when school was over and talk about soccer, each of us turning off when we neared our homes. It was so much fun. We all got comfortable soon because some were new to the school like me. We shared our culture with one another and enjoy hearing how each one of us used to live back home in his country.

Our relationships continued to flourish. After school, we used to play soccer and sometimes go the school gym and work out when time permitted.

51

Besides school, I was still working as a part-time employee at VIM on the weekends. I still kept in touch with Dr. Barry from Mount Vernon Neighborhood Hospital, visiting him occasionally. He introduced me to his colleague, Dr. Norah Farkouh. Dr. Farkouh is a very lovely and kind person; she is from Egypt. My relationships with these two doctors began to incline me toward a career in medicine. I have always loved little kids, so I was thinking about pursuing a career as a pediatrician. As the academic year ended, I was able to pass all my New York State Regents exams.

iv.   Summer 2011

That summer year was more fun for me. I had settled in; I understand American culture to some degree, and I had met some great people as well. I got an opportunity to work at Mount Vernon Neighborhood Hospital with Dr. Farkouh. As I have mentioned before, Dr. Farkouh is very kind, yet I was surprised when she presented me with this prospect. Since privacy is critical in the health industry, she would ask her patients first before she would allow me to stand by her side when she performed examinations: checking the ears, nose, eyes and heartbeat. After this, I would step out so she could talk privately with the patient. This was a learning opportunity for me.

I began to understand the job I would be doing if I opted to follow a career path in medicine. She taught me some critical aspects of the doctor's life. She used to show me all the books that she had to read after conferences so that she could use these new skills and treatments with her patients. Reading is a huge part of being a doctor. I did not enjoy reading that much, but if I wanted to pursue a career in medicine, I would have to get up to speed.

Dr. Farkouh saw my desire to learn, my passion, and my humility. As the summer was ending, she asked for my counselor's phone number. Dr. Farkouh wanted to discuss scholarship opportunities since I was going into my senior year and preparing to apply to college. The next day, I came in, and I immediately saw the anger and disappointment in her eyes. I asked, "Dr. Farkouh, are you okay?"

She looked at me and replied, "I cannot believe what your counselor told me after I asked her to help you apply for scholarships." I asked what my high school counselor said. Dr. Farkouh did not want to tell me, but I insisted, and she said, "Your high school counselor said you are an undocumented immigrant and therefore she cannot help you to apply for scholarships." It was a sad feeling, but I did not let that derail me from pursuing my career goals.

I was documented and had even acquired my US passport during the summer due to the Birth Abroad Act to a US Citizen Parent. A bit of history....This Act allows a child born abroad to US citizen parents who did not file a Birth Abroad Certificate with the US Consulate after birth to acquire automatic citizenship if the child enters the country before his or her eighteenth birthday. I came to America before turning eighteen years of age; therefore, when I applied for my US passport through my father, they gave it to me.

I didn't understand why my counselor would say something like that even though I used my green card to acquire my Social Security number before heading to Mount Vernon Board of Education. I think she should have known better, but what could I say as a young boy new in this country, trying to make it in America? My counselor was a Caucasian woman. Dr. Farkouh told me not to worry but, rather, to keep working hard. She said she would write me a letter of recommendation when I applied to college. I was still working at VIM to save money for college.

v.   12th Grade: Senior Year

My senior year in high school was a big moment in my life. I could have graduated in the summer by taking one class, but I opted to stay one more year to understand the college educational system better. Thankfully, I was assigned a new counselor name Peggy Williams. She was one of the most beautiful African American women I have ever encountered since I set my foot on American soil. She is an athletic woman with a big smile. Her personality sets her above most of her peers. Every student that I recall loved her.

Aside from that one remaining class, Spanish II, I enrolled in four AP classes: AP US History, AP Calculus, AP Statistics, and AP Biology. That year was going to be a lot harder on top of my job at VIM. I did not even know about standardized tests such as the SAT and ACT, which are required by most colleges in the US. My previous counselor never brought them up to me so that I could prepare because, in her mind, I was an undocumented immigrant, so why bother. Ms. Williams was shocked that my previous counselor never mentioned it to me. She got me up to speed and assigned me to a teacher who was great at prepping students for those tests.

In my AP classes, I met three boys; Nyako from Ghana; Lee, whose family came from South Korea, and Ma from China. These three guys were very hardworking students. I liked their mentality and attitude towards their academic work, so I started to hang out with them. Brian was the high school president. He worked closely with the school principal to resolve issues associated with student needs. His vision was very clear— strive for success—which made him one of the most respected students at the high school. Lee was a very smart guy and was projected to be either the valedictorian or salutatorian of our graduating class. Ma was a bright student with a dedicated career aspiration in finance. We used to do homework together and study for the upcoming test.

I remember one time, Lee, Ma, and I went to Koreatown and Chinatown to experience Asian culture. We had a great time. Something that stood out to me during this trip was an incident that took place in the NYC subway. During the subway ride, we were having a conversation and were laughing hard, making fun of each other. When I looked around, I saw people looking at us and starting to smile, wondering why we were having such a blast in the subway. It made me feel like maybe seeing three guys of different races having such so much fun together was something special.

Three of us were inducted into the National Honor Society chapter at the school. It was an amazing feeling, the day of our inauguration.

As time passed and I felt more comfortable at school, I asked my manager to allow me to work some days after school. He gave me Wednesdays and Fridays in addition to my weekend days. This brought additional dollars to my pockets as I started to save for college. It was a struggle, but I needed it.

I remember cramping up after coming from work especially on the weekends when I worked open to close, 9:30 am – 9:00 pm. Black Fridays were even worse. During the winter, we used to do universal inventory counts where selected employees from all VIM stores in New York and New Jersey would travel to different locations in a coach bus and scan all items using a barcode scanner. It was a good source of money because we work more than forty hours during the one-week inventory event. We were required to meet at a certain store location early in the morning, and if you showed up late, you would be asked to go home. I used to wake up early, around 4:00 am, get ready and walk 1.2 miles from my apartment to the train station on Dyer Avenue in the Bronx in a blizzard just make it on time. At that time, no buses were running. The train station was another nightmare because I did not know how it worked, so I had to ask for directions.

I took the opportunity to learn about the whole transportation system. After the inventory was over for the day, I would ride the train with some coworkers who lived in the Bronx; therefore, heading back home was not a hustle after work.

The sneaker game was hot around that time (2011-2014) with Nike being the dominant brand. I used to buy hot sneakers like Nike Jordan retro and Foamposite and resell them for higher prices. It was a good investment as I prepared for college. I had a lot going on at the time, but school was my priority. I learned how to manage my time wisely as I prepped for the standardized test.

vi.   Applying to College

I took the ACT and SAT and bombed the English section. I could not keep up with the pace of reading and answering the questions in a limited time. My scores were very bad and made Ms. Williams a bit concerned about me getting into a top college. By then, I knew how important these tests were. I had a good academic GPA, but my standardized test scores did not correlate well with my grades. I was very worried, wondering what I could have done differently to improve my test scores.

Ms. Williams worked tirelessly on my scholarship applications for college. I had explained my family situation to her and brought up the disastrous claim by my previous counselor about my immigration status. Ms. Williams had a bigger heart, and in every situation, she saw the bigger picture because of her experience as a teenager. I applied to colleges like Columbia, Cornell, NYU, Stony Brook, and City College of New York (CUNY). I believed I could compete; that's why I applied to some Ivy League schools. At that time, I was leaning towards medicine; therefore, I selected colleges with pre-med programs. Dr. Farkouh wrote me a letter of recommendation to support my college and scholarship applications.

One day, in my Spanish II class, I had finished our assigned task and then passed out because I was so exhausted from my part-time job. Ms. Williams was wrapping up a college scholarship application on my behalf. She needed some information from my end to finalize the paperwork. She came to my Spanish class because the deadline was approaching. Ms. Williams walked in, saw me asleep and then told my Spanish teacher, Ms. Tate, to call me outside. I remember a classmate sitting next to me tapped me to wake up. When I woke up, I was informed that my counselor was waiting for me outside in the hallway; I quickly got up and rushed outside. I was SHOCKED by what I saw; Ms. Williams was crying. I asked, "Ms. Williams, why are you crying?"

She looked at me and said, "Sam, you remind me of my past as a teenager when I used to work and go school at the same time. It was not easy, but I have faith in you that you will go far in life, so never give up and never stop your journey." That moment became part of me going forward. Ms. Williams seeing my dedication, kill-will mentality, hunger for success, desire to become somebody in the future gave me chills and goosebumps at the same time.

That moment gave me a new sense of belief. Someone like her had been in my situation many years ago and made it out. If it was possible for Ms. Williams to achieve her dream by overcoming obstacles that stood in her way, then it is possible for me as well.

I reserved her tears in front of me for special occasions when I have hit rock bottom. Meaning if I experience a roadblocks, and hell is raining down on me, feeling "I am not good enough" which may prompt me to quit how far I have come, her tears will energize me to even push and work harder. I went with her to complete the rest of my applications.

I remember my peers being accepted into bigger schools like Columbia, NYU, and Stanford University. Of my closest friends, Lee was accepted into business school at SUNY Binghamton University, Ma at New York City College, and Nyako at Manhattan College. Not only these universities but many more. On the other hand, I was still waiting to hear any acceptance from a college. I was getting rejection letters left and right. We had finished our AP exams in May and still no acceptance letter. The pressure built up as my classmates keep asking "any news, Sam," and my answer was "nope."

I had to remain patient and constantly remind myself not to worry. My overambitious choice of schools during my college applications put me in that situation.

Finally, the wait over! I was accepted into one of the CUNY schools: New City College of Technology (City Tech) in Brooklyn. To Lee and Ma, my school was deemed low compared to theirs. They even made some jokes about it, but I did not let that get under my skin. In every situation,

I always look at the bigger picture. I knew that after one year, I could always transfer to another college.

Because I did poorly on the English section on my SAT, I had to start summer school at City Tech.

I was placed in English for Speakers of Other Languages (ESOL) program to help me develop proficiency in grammar, speaking, reading, listening, and writing skills. Classes were scheduled threes time a week from 9:00 am to 12:00 pm. A placeholder was added to my account in terms of classes I could register for during the fall semester if I did not pass the CUNY Assessment Test at the end of the summer course. CUNY Assessment Tests (CATs) are designed to measure students' reading, writing, and mathematics skill before enrolling as a full-time student. If you don't pass, you have to take non-credit courses until you get up to speed.

vii.   Graduation Day

Graduation day felt different. All the work I had put in eventually paid off. I could not thank Ms. Williams enough for all her support and inspiration. My friends were very happy as well. We were all ready to start new chapters in our life. My father could not make it to my graduation due to his condition, but my mother and my half-brother did. Many parents congratulated me after the graduation event. I remember people from my block screaming "congratulations" from their apartment windows on our way back home. It was a great feeling. I reflected on my past from my genesis back in Ghana to now standing here. I graduated high school with rectitude as a member of the National Honor Society and was getting ready to start my new chapter at college in the fall.

I felt it all, most importantly, me and the people who believed in me. Dr. Farkouh, Dr. Barry, the amazing teachers and staff members at Mount Vernon High School. My mother always making sure that I could go to sleep after numerous cramps after long days at work. My father forcing me to be a man by constantly embedding the "get it or it will never happen" mentality into my brain. The emotions were tough to handle walking across the stage when my name was called, with the audience cheering. That moment helped to solidify my vision: you can achieve anything in life if your heart is set toward purpose. The mission was clear at this point: "Chasing and Catching the American Dream

PART – III

CHAPTER 5

PREPARING FOR COLLEGE

I was very busy during this time with a lot of decisions to make. My college was twenty-four miles from my town and unfortunately did not offer boarding. Commuting was a huge factor; I had to consider whether I should find a place to live closer to school. In addition to this, I had to take ESOL during the summer. I had to pass the CUNY Assessment Test in order to enroll as a full-time student. Since class started at 9:00 am, this gave me time to commute from Mount Vernon to City Tech in Brooklyn. I really enjoyed the summer class, which gave me a brief overview of how college works.

A reading assessment book used for the course was *Outliers: The Story of Success,* by Malcom Gladwell. For every session, a chapter of the book was assigned, and we would dissect it at the beginning of class. I learned plenty of lessons from that book and I used this knowledge to better myself moving forward. The "10,000-Hour Rule" was one of my favorite chapters; in order to succeed in life or anything that you choose to do, you have to be willing to put in the work. I knew from Africa that if I worked hard, one day I would become successful. I fancy hard work, as I have been grinding since the day I set my foot on American soil. "Winners don't sleep"; that was my mentality.

I had faith that, if I continued to put in the time and effort, I could achieve anything because that is what the American Dream is about: "Project Hard Work." The course ended and unfortunately, I was not able to pass the CUNY Assessment Test. Therefore, I had to retake it during fall semester, 2011. It was disappointing because my idea was to transfer to a different college after my first semester. I was only allowed to take calculus, physics, and the ESOL in the fall semester. Only calculus and physics were credits, and this would not be enough to allow me to transfer.

At the same time, I had started researching housing in New York. In my research, I came across The Towers at City College of New York housing. This building is located at 401 W 130th Street and is not far from City College. The building is more like a residence for students who go to City College. It also provides an additional housing service to all City University of New York (CUNY) students as well. I realize this was the best place for me to live because not only did it cut my commuting distance in half but also provided security, which was really good for my safety. The next phase was to find out the pricing for the housing. I booked an appointment to acquire information.

When I arrived, a nice woman name Atiya Patterson, who served as assistant director of housing at the Towers, met with me. My sense of humor took our conversation to a personal level. "Where are you from originally?" I asked, and she kindly replied, the Caribbean. I told her where I was from, and we had a few exchanges about our cultures. Then we returned our attention to the business at hand. I explained my situation and financial status to her. She understood and said she'd do her best to find the cheapest bedroom for me. I could have shared a bedroom with someone, but I opted to get my own room so that I could study at night.

All the paperwork went through, and Atiya found me a three-bedroom apartment with two other CUNY students. I was happy and anxious at the same time. Moving to a place to live with people that I hadn't met before was nerve-racking. I was wondering how they were going to welcome me when the move-in date arrived.

First time in my life living with strangers. The fears of what might lie ahead were getting hold of me. Were they going to be nice or mean? Would they clean up after themselves? I told myself to remain calm and see what happened because life is about getting comfortable being uncomfortable. I knew that if I transferred to another school, I would eventually live with other students, so this was the perfect opportunity to gain that experience of living with others.

The next decision that I had to make was my part-time job at VIM. The job was very reliable and had helped me save a lot of money for college. I wanted to continue working there. However, the distance from my new location posed a challenge. There are multiple locations across New York City, so I asked my new manager if I could transfer to a different location closer to the Towers.

At the time, my old manager, Amaudo, had been transferred to another location near the Towers at 571 W 181st St, New York. I went to his store to discuss the possibility of transferring to this location and working with Amaudo. Unfortunately, that did not work out, and I had to find the next closest to the Towers. I went to another location at 2239 Third Avenue, 122nd Street, New York, in East Harlem, and spoke to the manager. His name was Ali, and he was from Gambia in Africa. I had come across him once at the VIM location in Mount Vernon; he was filling in for Amaudo who was dealing with a family situation. The East Harlem location was one of the busiest VIM stores in New York City.

Ali agreed to transfer me and told me to work hard or I would be fired or returned to my old store in Mount Vernon. I replied with a smile, "No worries; you got it," and he smiled back, saying, "Good." Ali asked for my available date to start, and I said September (2012). Now I had found a place to live for college and saved my part-time job all by myself.

As the semester approached, I registered for classes: Calculus-1, Physics-1, and ESOL. My schedule was all over the place. My Calculus class was early in the morning, 8 am. My Physics I class was in the evening. I had it once a week, three hours on Wednesday from 6 pm to 9 pm. Some days I didn't have class, so I decided to work at VIM on those days to make some cash to buy my textbooks. I received a reminder email from Atiya.

I used the number 2 train to move my stuffs; I had two pieces of luggage. The Towers came furnished, so my two bags and my laptop were good. I purchased some cooking utensils, bedsheets, and pillows when I moved in, using my savings account. The rent wasn't cheap. I looked at my budget and how much money I had saved in my account. It wasn't enough to cover my rent. I was very worried, so I took out student loans to cover my rent.

CHAPTER 6

WHY AEROSPACE ENGINEERING

I n 2012, I saw on the local news about the NASA Space Shuttle Enterprise. We did not have cable and the television that my father had was an old plasma TV. We used an analog to digital converter box to help us watch the news. My mother used to watch the news every morning to catch up with the weather before heading out for work. It was a bit frustrating sometimes as the channel would scramble and you could miss out on some important event. I had to accept it because that was what we had at that time. I was closely following the Space Shuttle Enterprise journey to the Intrepid Sea, Air and Space Museum in New York City. I found it fascinating as the Enterprise sat on NASA's Boeing 747 Shuttle Carrier (SCA) to make its way to New York City.

The Enterprise never made it to space but served as a prototype that paved the way for the Space Shuttle program and numerous atmospheric test flights. These tests helped NASA to build the main Space Shuttles that transported American astronauts to the International Space Station (ISS).

On July 19, 2012, the Space Shuttle Pavilion on the Intrepid, featuring the Enterprise, was open to the public. I went there that day to see for myself. The line was long, but it was worth the wait. I saw the Enterprise with my naked eyes, and it was captivating. I was, like, something like this went to space and then came back to earth? I was in shock and it made me remember my first time in an airplane coming to America when I asked myself, "How is this piece of metal floating?" The United States is a land of knowledge. For those who choose to seek them, there will be solutions somewhere out there that can help them to transform or shape our world. It was quite extraordinary to watch the Enterprise.

There was a person giving a tour of the Enterprise. I asked him; what kind of degree do you have to acquire to build these things? He kindly replied aerospace and mechanical engineering. That day was SpaceFest, so I got a chance to talk to incredible people who work for NASA. I had heard of NASA, but I did not really understand what they do. July 19, 2012, answered most of my questions.

That day, I also learned about the NASA Mars Science Laboratory (MSL). The MSL is a robotic space probe known as the Curiosity. It was launched on November 26, 2011, by a rocket company named United Launch Alliance (ULA) and was scheduled to touch down on Mars in August, a nine-month journey. I remember asking one of the NASA representatives from Jet Propulsion Laboratory (JPL) about the mission of the Curiosity, which includes climate change, the habitability of Mars, geology, and most importantly, extracting data for a future manned mission to Mars.

She was an amazing woman with an Indian heritage. She took her time to explain the overall objectives of Curiosity, and I was very impressed. I also remember having a conversation with another man working for NASA. I asked him where he went to college and his field of study. He answered aerospace engineering; he obtained his bachelor's and master's degrees from the University of Michigan. He also gave me advice about pursuing a career in the field of mechanical and aerospace engineering. It's important to acquire a master's degree if you can, he said. I received many posters including the Curiosity, the

Shuttle Carrier, the Orion Spacecraft that will carry future astronauts to space and beyond, and a poster of former African American NASA astronaut Leland Devon Melvin.

After gathering plenty of information at the event, I called it a day—one that filled my heart with joy. At that moment, I decided to pursue a career in either mechanical or aerospace engineering instead of medicine. I had never thought about becoming an astronaut, but that day made it an option.

The next few days, I started researching the differences between mechanical and aerospace engineering. After my research, I chose aerospace engineering because I wanted to learn about aircraft and spacecraft and be part of a team that builds the latter. The next phase was to start considering universities that offered aerospace engineering in New York State.

My reason to limit my search to New York was financial constraint. I didn't want to lose TAP, which is a tuition assistance program for New York State residents. After my search, I narrowed it down to Cornell and Syracuse University. I had already applied to Cornell during my senior year and been rejected for their pre-med program. This time, I decided to apply to their mechanical and aerospace engineering program, and I did the same for

Syracuse University. My idea was to transfer after my first year at City College of Technology (City Tech).

CHAPTER 7

STARTING COLLEGE AT THE CITY COLLEGE OF TECHNOLOGY IN BROOKLYN NEW YORK

i.   Fall 2012

The vision for my first full semester was pre-determined due to the outcome of my CUNY Assessment Test during the summer. I had to study extra hard to pass it this time around to enroll in more than two credited classes. I finally met my roommates, two Caucasian students, James and Brian. They were very welcoming. Both were New Yorkers as well. James was born and raised in Staten Island, and Brain was from Brooklyn. James was studying architecture at one of those CUNY schools, the name of which I can't remember.

Brian was studying physics at City College of New York, which was like six to ten minutes walking distance from the towers. Brain didn't have to worry about dealing with public transportation.

My first class was Calculus-I, offered at 8:30 am Mondays and Wednesdays. All my professors were awesome and very helpful. I remember my ESOL professor's name, Yvonne Goldson. At the beginning of her class, I explained my situation to her, how I needed to utilize all available resources to help me pass the CUNY Assessment Test at the end of the semester. All my classes were very small, and it was easier to participate during lectures

James was never home due to his area of study. Brian, on the other hand, I spent a lot of time with. We were both taking Calculus-1 and Physics-1 during the fall semester. We had plenty of discussions on topics we were currently learning in school and even solved some homework problems together. Brian was a smart guy, and I got a chance to learn plenty of basic physics tricks from him. I remember sometimes he would come back from a lecture and ask, "Hey, Sam, do you want to see something cool?" I would reply, "Yes." He would then go ahead and perform a science experiment he just learned during his physics lab.

It was so much fun! In my opinion, physics is one of the best way to understand how our universe operate and this fascinates me a lot.

Later in the semester, my physics professor informed me that he had spoken to our department chair about me tutoring high school physics. It caught me off guard because I wasn't expecting this kind of consideration from my professor. It was a very generous offer. It made me realize that when you work hard, people notice it, and that could make a lot of difference in your life. I was a good student in his class. Unfortunately, I respectfully declined his offer because I was making good money at VIM, and it fit my schedule well. I didn't feel the need to get another job.

In addition, I needed to devote any extra time that I had to study and practice in my ESOL class for my assessment test. He understood. He was a very kind person as well. We used to take the A/E train together at Jay Street Metro Tech in Brooklyn after class around 9:20 pm. Sometimes, we would have a conversion about current topics that we were discussing in class. I even asked for his opinion about pursuing a career in aerospace engineering. He told me that I could do it if I continued my work ethic.

I shared the same thoughts with my calculus teacher about transferring to either Syracuse or Cornell University in the spring semester to pursue a career in aerospace engineering. His concern was the cost because these two universities were private institutions. I told him that I was willing to take on the debt load in order to achieve my dream. He understood my passion and wished me best of luck.

I began the college transfer applications process. I called my high school counselor, Ms. Williams, and informed her about my decision to transfer to one of these two universities. She sent my high school transcript and my standardized test scores to both schools as I requested. I also sent my mid-term grades to both universities' admissions committees. I received a second rejection letter from Cornell University, and I was very disappointed. It was hard as I kept on failing. Failing is tough for everyone. Sometimes I even asked myself "is this journey worth it".

These failures drained a lot of energy out me. I remember asking myself "why always me", "Am I not working hard enough?", "what else am I doing wrong?" and plenty more of these rhetorical questions as my frustrations hanged-on to grow but through all, I kept my composure, stayed positive and continued to work hard. My application for admission to Syracuse was still pending, as it was missing some important documents. I did my best to streamline the admission process by retrieving the missing documents, but it was too late for them to make a decision. I received a letter later stating that they would consider me for the fall 2013 semester instead. This letter gave me hope and made me realize that I had a chance at this university. I informed Ms. Williams about both outcomes, and she told me to keep her in the loop and stay positive during the process.

As the semester went on, I started looking into first-year classes for aerospace engineering students at Syracuse University. The idea was to take spring semester classes similar to the ones offered at Syracuse. I figured this was a smart thing to do, as it would increase my overall chance of being accepted for the fall 2013 semester if the admission committee saw my grades for those classes.

It may seem like I was getting ahead of myself, but I was highly focused on my education and willing to do whatever it took to get to the finish line. I had this road map laid out prior to the beginning of my first semester at City Tech. As the fall 2012 semester ended, I passed all three classes. Passing ESOL paved the way for me to register for classes as a full-time student. I was behind schedule and, therefore, I decided to take six classes to catch up as a freshman.

ii.   Spring 2013

This semester was very difficult. I had register for six classes. I knew that I had to work hard to pass all the classes with flying colors in order to have a chance at getting into Syracuse University for the upcoming fall semester. I learned to manage my time wisely and even cut the hours at my part-time job. This was hard because I had to find other ways to increase my income.

Knowing that fashion was a huge part of the New York City lifestyle, I explored the possibility of raising revenue by working in this field. I decided to invest a certain percentage of my money into reselling Nike basketball sneakers.

A special retail name House of Hoops that is part of Foot Locker was not too far from the CCNY Towers. It is located at 268 W. 125th Street, New York. This special store always received all the Nike basketball limited-release shoes in great quantity. I decided to purchase a decent amount and resell them on eBay. In addition to this, I established a business partnership with a small retail store, Dynasty Urbanwear on Gramatan Avenue in Mount Vernon, NY. The owner of this store came from Ghana, so it was nice to do business with him. I would sell some of my sneakers to him, and he would deposit the money in my bank account. This was greatly to my advantage in terms of making a profit and gave me enough time to study.

About a month into the semester, my father's condition got worse, and he spent almost six weeks at the hospital. My mother was very stressed; I could see it in her face. I prayed for him to get better every day before I went to bed. Later, he was taken to the nursing home after his condition improved. I remembered visiting him at the nursing home; I was very sad and struggled to eat when I came home for a couple of days.

This semester turned out to be tough because I almost lost track of my academics due to my family situation, but I stayed positive through all and continued with my schoolwork.

After my mid-term grades came in, I informed the registrar's office to send an official copy of my transcript to Syracuse University. This turned out to be a dead end, as the admission committee at Syracuse kept sending me emails about my missing mid-term grades. It was very frustrating.

I took matters into my own hands by asking the registrar office to give me a sealed envelope with a copy of my official transcript inside. I will mail it myself. It caused a huge fight. They were hesitant to do it this way, but later one person agreed to my request. I was willing to do whatever it took to streamline my transfer process.

As the semester wound down, I decided to register for Chemistry-I for the summer. My decision to do this was based on Syracuse's first-year class requirements for engineering students.

Back to my family side, my father did not like it at the nursing home and wanted to go back to Ghana instead. He opposed the treatments getting at the nursing home. He felt going back to Ghana would be beneficial to his health and happiness as his family members will take care of him properly compared to what he was receiving from the nurses.

This desire to go back home grew exponentially as the days passed. It put a lot of pressure on my mother. She knew that if he went back, he might not get the same treatment as in the United States, putting his health at risk, but he insisted. I second my mother's thoughts but we could not convinced him to stay in the States.

My mother had to agree along with my half-siblings in the States. They arranged his departure for Ghana. My mother and my half-sister would travel with him. I went back to Mount Vernon to assist with the transition process, such as buying things he would use in Ghana.

During this period, I was also preparing for finals. This was a crucial moment in my life. I needed to pass all my classes with a minimum grade of B in order to increase my chances at Syracuse University. I was going through many emotions because of my father's condition, but I didn't let it overwhelm the task at hand, my academic success.

I received my scores at the end of my finals, and I passed all my classes with excellence. I went back to the registrar's office and asked for my official transcript to be send to Syracuse University. I spoke to the same woman who worked at the registrar's office during my previous quarrel with them. She told me to come back in two days and it would be ready. She was very kind.

Two days later, I went back and it was ready. I went straight to the post office to mail it express. Three days later, I called the admission's office at Syracuse University to find out if they had received it. I was informed that everything had been received and they were ready to process my application.

At this point, all that I could do then was wait for their answer. I began to prepare and purchase the entire necessary supplements for my chemistry-I class in the summer.

iii.   Summer 2013

My chemistry class kicked off well in June. It was a small class with all the students pursuing a career in healthcare except me. I really enjoyed the class and got a chance to interact with the professor often. At the same time, I was very anxious, waiting to hear back from Syracuse University. I remember checking my email every couple of minutes.

About mid-June, in class, I saw an email notification on my phone and quickly opened it. That moment turned out to be one of the best in my life. It was an acceptance letter from Syracuse University College of Engineering and Computer Science! I was filled with joy. I tried hard to hold in my celebration because I was still in class. Classmates who were sitting close to me noticed something was up with me. They asked, "Are you okay?" I told them what had happened. They all congratulated me and were very happy as well.

That moment reaffirmed my conviction to never give up. After class, I called Ms. Williams and shared this great news. She was in tears and even struggled to speak. It was very emotional. I thanked her for all her support and for not giving up on me. It was not easy trading emails and phone calls among the admission offices, Ms. William and me.

Brian was very interested in my application to Syracuse University. So when the news broke, I informed him as well. He was very happy for me and wished me the best of luck. I was accepted late; therefore, there was no space in the dormitory. The admissions office suggested a list of off-campus housing with contact information for someone to assist me in finding housing. I passed my chemistry-I class as well.

After this great news, I decided to get a second job because VIM was very slow, and I was not getting enough hours. I figured that the second job would help me cover all my expenses as I transitioned from New York City to

Syracuse in upstate New York. I was informed about Craigslist by my friends, so I started looking for a position in sales. I found a couple and filled out an applications. About a week later, I received a call from Paul, who was a manager for a SalesMakers, Inc. We scheduled an interview at one of the Starbucks locations on 42nd street in Manhattan. The interview went well, and Paul did a fantastic job explaining the duties of my position.

I got hired and became a sales rep for Duracell Powermatt at Queens Center Mall in New York. We had a kiosk in the food court at the mall where we sold this new technology to customers. In 2013, Duracell Powermatt was the newest technology on the market. It offers wireless charging capability via electromagnetic induction. Some of the commercial videos that we used to show the customers to increase sales featured Hip-Hop icon Jay-Z utilizing this technology to charge his cell phone.

It was a good source of income, as I got commissions based on the amount of product that I sold on top of my hourly rate. We used to travel to street fairs in Mid-town New York City to make sales. I had a great time during these events. New York City is a huge tourist destination, so during these street fairs, I got a chance to talk to people from around the world.

As I mentioned, I am a big fan of soccer, and in Europe, the sport is very popular. I knew many famous soccer players around the world. So when these customers approached our table and I heard their accent, I would ask, "Are you from [European country]?" I was right most of the time. I would then go ahead and mention a famous soccer player from their respective country. The international customers were very surprised and asked, "How do you know that?" I would kindly reply, "Because I'm a soccer fan and Liverpool FC is my team."

Liverpool FC is one of the most decorated and well-respected soccer team in England with a worldwide fan base. Sometimes I would let them know I was born in Ghana, which is also a huge soccer country. Not to mention how they beat the United States Men's Soccer Team twice in two consecutive World Cups (2006, 2010). The United States got their revenge in 2014 World Cup. It was indeed a great experience!

My father was still preparing to go back to Ghana. I was nervous about his condition. I told my mother about transferring schools. She did not know Syracuse, but she agreed with my decision. They departed in July 2013.

I had to find a place to live in Syracuse for the upcoming fall semester. I contacted one of the off-campus housing realtors and scheduled an appointment to check out a place. I spoke to a woman who was in charge of showing the properties to students; her name was Stephanie. She was very nice and kind, so we arranged a time for me to book a trip to Syracuse and check out the properties. I didn't know anything about Syracuse except the university, which I had never visited in person.

I took a one-day trip to Syracuse to meet Stephanie. I found out that Greyhound and Amtrak go to Syracuse. Since the bus was the cheapest option, I purchased a ticket for Greyhound. My bus departed around 5:30 am from the Port Authority Bus Terminal in New York City. I arrived at Syracuse at roughly 11:00 am. Stephanie picked me up at the bus station. She showed me a couple of properties they owned, and I decided to go with the cheapest one close to campus. We drove by campus via Comstock Avenue to get a glimpse of my new school. Her schedule was tight, so I could not tour the campus even though I wanted to.

After my appointment was over, I had some hours left before my bus depart for New York City. I wasn't familiar with the campus, which was huge compared to City Tech (my formal college in Brooklyn). Therefore, I didn't feel the need to walk around without a tour guide. Stephanie recommended Destiny USA, which one of the best malls in the United States, as a place to kill the remaining time before my departure around 9 pm. The mall was a few minutes away from the bus station.

I remember grabbing lunch and going to the movies. I saw *Pacific Rim,* featuring one of the biggest movie stars, Idris Elba, which was released on July 13, 2013, in IMAX. That was my first time seeing a movie on such a big screen. Then it was time to go. I took the Greyhound back to New York City.

As the summer was ending, I was getting ready for my journey to Syracuse. I told Atiya at the CCNY Towers about my transfer. She wished me the best of luck, and I thanked her for all the love and generosity she showed during this part of my journey. I moved out of the building when my one-year lease ended.

For the rest of the summer, I lived at Mount Vernon by myself because my parents had left for Ghana. I made all the necessary preparations for my transition. As the time to leave for Syracuse got closer, I started having mix feelings. I was very excited to start a new chapter of my life at this University but at the same time, I was nervous and worried about loneliness. Especially meeting the right students who share the same vision as mine "dream catchers". Part of me said "do not worry you will do great" because this is not the first time going through such thing.

PART – IV

CHAPTER 8

WALKING THE WALK: LIFE AT SYRACUSE, UPSTATE NEW YORK

On August 12, 2013, I moved to Syracuse. Classes begin on the 19th. I had three suitcases with me. I took a taxi from Mount Vernon to Port Authority Bus Terminal in New York City and then hopped on Greyhound. The bus terminal was very busy around that time because students are heading back to college in upstate New York. It was a huge transition, but I was ready for the new challenge. I called my mother, who was in Ghana, and informed her about everything. I arrived at the bus station in Syracuse and took a taxi to my apartment.

Prior to my arrival, I arranged a time window with Stephanie to meet me at my new apartment so that I could get the keys. I was the second roommate to arrive. It was a four-bedroom apartment. My roommates were all transfer students as well. The next day, my roommate Jacob and I went to Walmart to buy school supplies. Neither of us had a car so we took public transportation. I remember trying to use my New York City MTA MetroCard on a Syracuse public bus. The bus driver looked at me and said, "Sir, we do not use these here; we have our own version." My roommate had additional quarters, so he was able to spot me. The following day we went to campus. There was a lot going on including freshmen orientation and transfer students meetup activities.

I remember visiting my school, College of Engineering and Computer Science, for the first time. I met a young lady, Breezy Knight, who was sitting in front of Link Hall facing the quad. Breezy was also a transfer student with an associate's degree from a community college. She transferred to Syracuse University to complete her bachelor's in mechanical engineering. We had a great conversion and became close friends.

About three days later, our new roommate, Anthony Moretti, arrived. His family came from Italy. Moretti was

94

a veteran who had served in the Navy in Japan. After he got out of the service, he decided to pursue a career in finance at Whitman School of Management at Syracuse University.

The University offers a veterans program for men and women. I gave him huge respect and thanked him for his service. Stephanie later informed us that there would be no more joining us. Therefore, we had one additional room left.

The weekend before my first class, we went out to Marshall Street, which is a place where they have bars for the college students, to grab a few drinks. We went to a bar called Chucks, which is one of the famous bars in the history of Syracuse University.

That night, we met two additional transfer students, Gabriel Shepherd and Anthony Pegues. Gabriel grew up in Beaver Falls in Upstate New York. He studied Business Administration at Jefferson Community College. Pegues was also a veteran who served in Iraq during the war in the 2000s. He transferred from a small community college in Upstate New York to study accounting at Whitman School of Management.

My transition from New York City to Syracuse was off to a great start. At that time, my accent was still very thick;

Anthony loved it and so did the rest of my new friends. They all used to repeat everything that I said. Anthony Pegues is a tall guy, six feet and seven inches. Anthony Moretti is around five feet and seven inches. The height differential between these two veterans was huge. Calling both of them by their first names was very confusing at times during our conversations. Therefore, to distinguish between the two, I proposed to call Pegues; Big Tony and Moretti; Little Tony. Both were super cool when I decided to call them by these names. I remember Big Tony laughing at my accent the whole night.

CHAPTER 9

LIFE AT SYRACUSE UNIVERSITY

i.   Sophomore Year Fall 2013

The first day of classes was a different feeling. Pumped up and at the same time anxiety-producing. New environment, bigger campus compared to what I have seen before. A normal lad trying to make it in America. I had nobody to look up to; my intellect and vision had gotten me thus far. My hunger for success was the advance propulsion system that I relied on starting a new chapter in my journey. In my first class, the professor allowed each of us to introduce ourselves. I was very surprised during the introductions because the class was composed of students from all over the country, not only New Yorkers as at City Tech.

I got my entire syllabus after two days of classes, listing all the textbooks required for the semester. I went to the bookstore the next day to see if I could purchase these books. I was shocked at the prices; I couldn't afford most of them. I had a little money left in my bank account as a safety net, and did not want to spend all of it on textbooks. If something happened, any kind of financial emergency, I wanted to be able to support myself. So, I began to ponder...how am I going to get my hands on these books? To get around this, I used to borrow some of the textbooks from the library, the most expensive ones.

My previous college, City Tech, was relatively small compared to Syracuse University. I had to walk to a different building for my next class. I felt like a freshman because I was always asking for directions. Syracuse University is a big campus.

My schedule was all over the place because of the classes I took at City Tech; therefore, I was placed in some junior level classes as well as my standard sophomore classes. It was very tough. I didn't know anyone to study with or do homework with. I remember being late for most of my classes because I couldn't find the building.

Since classes were held in auditoriums, I decided to sit in the front row. This allowed me to engage in one-on-one conversation with the professors. As classes progressed, I made friends in my engineering school. I met a guy named Teddy Belay, studying mechanical engineering. Teddy approached me one day after class and introduced himself. "Hey, what's up....I notice that you were not part of our freshmen class (2012); are you a transfer student?" he asked.

I replied, "Yeah, just transferred from City Tech in Brooklyn."

He said, "Oh, I'm from Brooklyn... I notice that you have an accent."

"Yeah, I was born in Ghana."

"Cool. My family came from Ethiopia, but I was born in Brooklyn."

The kindness that Teddy showed was extraordinary. He welcomed me as a brother from another mother, and through him, I went on to meet many more students, including his roommate, Evan Brown from Massachusetts, who was studying international relations and some other engineering students like Joel Rosado from Pennsylvania. Evan was a very nice Caucasian guy who enjoyed soccer like me. We used to talk about the English Premier League all the time. Joel, on the other hand, had a similar story to mine.

He was the first kid in his Spanish family to go to college and he had to overcome much adversity to get to Syracuse University. It was such an inspiring story. Joel is a humble and very fun person. His story made us connect on a personal level, and we ended up becoming close friends.

I only had one class with Teddy even though we were both in our sophomore year. That sums up how weird my schedule was because I was ahead in terms of classes. Mechanical and aerospace engineering students take similar classes until their senior year. I was missing a few key freshman classes for engineering students; therefore, I had to take those during my sophomore year.

I had to find a way to sustain myself financially. I chose not to work part-time during my first semester. I wanted to maximize my studying time so that I could achieve a high GPA in my first semester. My GPA from City Tech did not transfer.

My sneakers business philosophy was still in hand, so one day I decided to check out the mall, Destiny USA. I discovered that many of the sneaker retail stores like Champs Sports, Footlocker House of Hoops, Finish Line and other small stores had newly released sneakers that had sold out in New York City because the demand was so high. I took advantage of this by buying sneakers and shipping them to Dynasty Urbanwear on Gramatan Avenue in Mount Vernon using a portion of my safety net money. I realized it was a great way to grow that money. It was a good source of income.

Nike dropped the Jordan's Retro 10 in white and black during the fall season. My business partner told me to buy selected sizes, as many as I could, because it was in high demand among his customers in New York City as the release day approached. I had the money to buy about twenty pairs. I asked my roommate Little Tony to see if he could drive me to the mall early in the morning before 8 am, but unfortunately, he had errands he had to run.

I then turned my attention to Breezy Knight; she had a car. Thankfully, she lived a few blocks away from my apartment. I explained what I was trying to do, and she offered to help me. When the release date arrived, she picked me up at my place, which was about seven blocks from her apartment, and drove me to the mall. I was able to purchase more than twenty pairs and ended up selling some even at the mall to some folks who did not get the size they were looking for. I remember Breezy appreciating my business plan as a genius way to make money as a college student.

After that, we drove to the US post office on Marshall Street to ship everything to Dynasty Urbanwear. I continued this scheme to help sustain myself financially. Sometimes, I had to take public transportation because I couldn't get anyone to drive me to the mall. On those occasions, I would buy a few pairs that I could carry and ship them as usual at Marshall Street.

As the semester wound down, I got a taste of Syracuse winter weather. Little did I know; I thought the weather here was the same as New York City and therefore my jackets and sweaters would be good enough to keep me warm. I didn't prepare for the monstrous winter storms in Upstate New York. I got severely sick. My mother, back in the States from Ghana, would call every weekend to check on me. I remember my roommate Little Tony knocking at my door in the middle of the night to make sure that I was okay. I appreciated the love that my brother showed during such a difficult time. When I finally got back on my feet, he decided to take me to Destiny USA to get some winter clothes.

I had to walk in this snow about twenty minutes to get to class. The severity of the winter weather increased as the semester reached an end. I couldn't bear it anymore, so I decided to opt out of my lease and seek campus housing.

As the semester ended, I distributed all my belongings among my friends. Teddy and Evan took the majority of them and then gave the remainder to other friends that I had met in Syracuse. I went back home to Mount Vernon for the winter break.

My final grades came in, and I didn't do as well as I expected. My GPA did not meet my standards. I told myself to work harder next semester. I went back to work at VIM in Harlem to make some money before returning to Syracuse for the spring semester. During that time, I used to wake up early in the morning to take the route 42 bus from New Rochelle to Wakefield 241st Street in White Plain and then hop on the number 2 train to East 180th Street, Morris Park, in the Bronx to catch the 5 train to 125th and Lexington Avenue for work. It was not an easy commute.

ii.   First Year: Sophomore Spring 2014

In the spring semester, I moved to south campus. It was a two-bedroom apartment that shared a common space with my assigned roommate. I visited my friends to pick up all my belongings. It was a huge relief to settle into my new place. It was very expensive, but I took on more student loans to facilitate my housing. The shuttle buses to class were very reliable. I set a higher goal for myself by doing well in my classes compared to the previous semester.

Textbooks were very expensive. I remember having a conversation with Teddy about the possibility of finding additional resources to help with my textbooks. He introduced me to Syracuse University CSTEP program. CSTEP stands for The Collegiate Science and Technology Entry Program. It is designed for students from economically disadvantaged or historically underrepresented backgrounds (African American, Hispanic, Pacific Islander, etc.).

The aim of CSTEP is to help students succeed by providing the necessary academic support such as counseling and mentorship, financial support to purchase textbooks, Graduate Record Examinations (GRE) tutoring and much more. The next few days, I went there to learn more about this amazing program. Their office was located on the second floor of Bowne Hall. I signed in at the front desk as instructed. A few minutes later, my name was called, and I met Douglas Wandersee, an academic service coordinator for CSTEP. Douglas welcomed me warmly and went on to explain the overall mission of CSTEP. He was able to help me with some of my textbooks. On top of this, we scheduled a time to discuss my academic performance every two weeks. My semester was off to a great start.

Two of the classes that I enjoyed the most were Thermodynamics and Solid Mechanics. Two amazing professors, Dr. Ben Akih-Kumgah and Dr. Alan Levy, respectively, taught these classes. Dr. Ben was born in Africa like me and was very inspirational. Dr. Levy was from Coney Island, Brooklyn, and had that New York City vibe. I remember sitting in the front seat all the time in Dr. Levy's class and asking plenty of questions because I enjoyed his class. I also made the best use of their office hours to get one-on-one explanations about some of the topics that came up in the lectures.

As the semester progressed, I started looking into the possibility of working with a professor during the summer. I discussed this idea with my academic advisor, and he introduced me to the Research Experience for Undergraduates (REU) offered at Syracuse University during the summer. Since I hadn't taken any advanced engineering courses, it was a little bit harder to get a professor to work with. Not only that, but there were limited funds for this summer program.

Professors usually selected students, mostly juniors and seniors, who could contribute to their lab by working with PhD candidates. I had a conversation with Dr. Ben about working in his lab. Funding was scarce, but I was doing well in his class, so he employed me as an independent study student to assist in a portion of his research studies. I was very happy to enter the research field.

As the semester reclined, I signed up for two summer classes, one in social science and one in critical research and writing. The main idea behind these two summer classes was to boost my total GPA before heading into my junior year. When the semester ended, I moved out from south campus to our main campus dormitory, Haven Hall, for my summer classes. I didn't go back to New York City.

iii.   First Year: Sophomore Summer 2014

I kicked off my first summer in Syracuse brightly. The campus looked super amazing during summer. It was mesmerizing. Green grasses and flourishing tress everywhere. I felt connected to the Mother Nature as never before in the United States. I started to reminisce about growing up in Ghana. Waking up to, the green trees every morning with a fresh air is something that I will always cherish about the Mother Land and its beautiful tropical weather. I picked my classes to span both summer sessions (I & II). That is, I took critical research and writing in summer session-I from May to June, followed by my social science class from July to August in session-II. This spacing allowed me to devote most of my time to my independent research with Dr. Ben. I was very excited to work with him on a research project. My task was to assist in studying thermal instability in aviation fuel.

I was responsible for researching the fuel production process and investigating the additives added to the fuel to improve its efficiency. I also examined how these fuels got approved by the America Society for Testing and Materials (ASTM) to power aircraft. Besides this, I also analyzed the elements that initiate chemical reactions in aviation fuel. This experience allowed me to expand my knowledge horizon. I gained a better insight into different types of aviation fuels, for both commercial and military applications; some of the challenges facing the production lines, and the current solutions in place to combat those issues.

My first summer session class was going well. I learned about research techniques, which, in turn, assisted me in my independent study. We engaged in high-level selected topics and were even assigned into groups sometimes to work on a project. The pace was very smooth, and the professor was great as well. I passed the class. I had about a week before starting my second session.

Before the end of my first session, I was looking for an off-campus housing closer to campus. I found a place, on Ackerman Ave, which was a very popular area for Syracuse University students. It was a two-story house with four bedrooms available on the first floor. I needed additional people to sign the lease with me.

I contacted Moretti (Little Tony), Pegues (Big Tony), and Shepherd. Pegues was working in Syracuse, but both Moretti and Shepherd were back in their hometowns for the summer break. Unfortunately, Pegues had recently signed a new lease somewhere further away from campus because he had a car. However, Moretti and Shepherd were both available to sign the lease with me. It all worked out well after I spoke with the property owner. I was very happy because not only did it cut my housing costs in half but it was also closer to my school (College of Engineering and Computer Science). I moved into my new place at the beginning of my second summer session. I remember Pegues visiting me one day. He said,

"Yo, Sam, I think it's better to get a bike because it will be easier to get to places."

I replied, "Yea, you are right, dude, how much are they?"

"Not that expensive; we can get a cheap one at Walmart."

Pegues (Big Tony) then drove me to Walmart to get a bike so that I could go to a grocery shopping without waiting for any public transportation. I enjoy cooking my own food. That bike was nice, lime green and white with dual suspension, front and back, and another shock absorber for my seat. That bike was my Ferrari! This made my life a bit easier because I could get to places quickly. I rode that bike everywhere I went, including downtown Syracuse to watch the fireworks during the July 4th celebration.

My second session class was going well. It was a lot of reading, as you can imagine, a full semester course compacted into four weeks. As the session approached an end, so did my summer research. All summer undergraduates' research participants were required to prepare a presentation as a recap of what they did during the research period.

It was fascinating to learn more about other people's work and the kind of research that each faculty was involved in. This was a huge advantage because it gave me a new perspective on a field that I could specialize in if I opted to go to graduate school. I passed this session's class as well. These two classes raised my overall academic GPA. After everything was over, I went back to New York City for about two weeks to spend time with my mother before heading back for my junior year fall semester.

iv.   Second Year: Junior Fall 2014

This semester was a pivotal moment as I continued to push harder in my journey. My father's condition—he was now back in Ghana—was getting worse. I had already set a higher goal for myself in terms of doing well in my upcoming classes. I registered for four classes. I was good at mathematics, so I decided to minor in math. I enrolled in a partial differential equation course after discussing it with my advisor. He warned me about the difficulties I might encounter because it was an advanced mathematics class (graduate level).

My sneaker business had slowed down, and I chose not to invest my time in it anymore. I had to find an alternative way to make money. I looked into student work-study, which comes with your FAFSA when you apply for financial aid. I ended up applying for many different jobs on campus, including the Carrier Dome sports stadium. About a week and half prior to the beginning of this semester, I received a job offer at the Carrier Dome as a concession runner.

My primary duties were to restock all the stands that sold beer and food during sports events and concerts. Syracuse University is a huge athletic school, so I was very excited about it. I would get the chance to work at all the seasonal games, both football and basketball. Time management became crucial this semester. I was nervous but at the same time ready for the contest. I believed that I could do it big.

Once the semester started, I went back to Douglas at the CSTEP office. I explained everything to him, including my father's condition. He was very worried about his prognosis, which affected my academic performance. I told Douglas I would do my best to stay focused in class. He suggested checking on me every two weeks to see how I was performing in my classes. I thanked him for his dedication. The semester started very well and even wanted to continue my summer research, but

111

unfortunately, I did not have any additional time to devote to this work.

One class that exposed me to practical engineering applications was my Mechanical and Aerospace Engineering Laboratory. This class is taught by one of the most successful professors in the field of fluid dynamics in the United States, Dr. Mark Glauser. This particular class exposes undergraduate engineering students to the application of Solid Mechanics, Signal Processing, Vibrations, and Fluid Mechanics. I enjoyed this class because I was able to get a perspective on how to apply the theories learned in my other classes to actual engineering problems. It has a workload, as all mechanical and aerospace engineering students at Syracuse University will agree. After performing various experiments in the lab, calculations are due in the first week followed by a full lab report in the second week. I learned so much from this class. I used to ask questions all the time and utilized Dr. Glauser's office hours regularly. We developed a good relationship, and I ended up learning more about his research area as well.

The semester ended, and I passed all my classes with flying colors. I made it onto the Dean's List in our department that semester. Not only did I make this list, but I also received a certificate of outstanding achievement from CSTEP, the highest honor a student can receive in each semester. My confidence grew because I had achieved the goals I set for myself. Douglas was very happy for me and told me to continue my hard work.

I chose not to go back home for the winter break but rather work at the Carrier Dome to make some money before spring semester. I did inform my mother about this decision, and she was okay with it. My mother always supported my vision. I supported her financially to assist my siblings back in Ghana, using part of my safety net account. The workload was too much for her, and so she was open to allowing me to work and provide financial support. Four kids plus the extended family needs back in Ghana, well you can imagine, that was too tough for her to handle it alone financially.

Something unique and beautiful about my mom is that, she always smiles. No matter what her situation is, positive or negative. For that reason, if she doesn't tell you what her problems are, you would never guess she is going through a difficult time. She is very generous person and always willing to help others in needs back in Ghana.

CHAPTER 10

THE UNEXPECTED

i.   Second Year: Junior Spring 2015

I had huge momentum going into this semester. I had finally settled into the academic style at Syracuse University. I had also made some friends to study and do homework with. I signed up for five classes. During the first week of class, I went back to Douglas to go over my schedule and so he could assist me with my textbook purchases from the bookstore at Schine Student Center. He was able to provide me with financial support to rent textbooks. The rest I was able to get used ones online. I was off to a great start.

About a week and a half into the semester, my mother called me while I was heading to my next class and informed me that my father had passed away. It was a shocking and devastating moment in my life. It was very hard to digest what had happened to my family. I was worried the day he left the United States because he was not fully recovered. The stroke and diabetes kept on weakening him. I had prayed to God to prolong his life so that I could fully take care of him once I become somebody. I wanted to prove to him that I was going to be great, make it in America someday and take care of my siblings and my mother.

All those visions of mine were cut short. I thought he was going to return from Ghana in a much healthier condition because he believed the traditional herbal medicine would heal him. He was tired of taking insulin shots every day to maintain his sugar level. I remember going to my next class and paying zero attention to what the professor was lecturing on. Following that class, I went back to my apartment and stayed in for the rest of the day. I skipped all my remaining classes.

The next day, I went back to Douglas to inform him about what had just happened. I saw the sadness in his face as he offered his condolences. I remember him asking if I needed to take the semester off to spend some time with my family. I told him that I would speak to my mother first to see if she needed my company at this difficult time.

On the phone, she was very emotional, and I felt her pain. She encouraged me to stay in school and work hard.

Our extended family back in Ghana was making the necessary preparations to hold his funeral service. In our culture, you can preserve a dead body as long as you wish to make the necessary preparations before burial. I told my mother to keep me informed with how things were propagating back in Ghana.

The semester turned out to be tough. I lost focus in most of my lectures. My friends asked me if I was doing okay. I told them about my father's death, and they all offered to help me if I needed anything. I really appreciated all of their support at such a difficult time. I remember Douglas checking in on me every week to see how I was doing. I could not thank him enough for all his support.

About a week later, my mother called and informed me the date of my father's funeral service. The family chose June because they believed this would give my family in America time to save money to better prepare for a final goodbye to our father.

After my mother told me the decision, I said it would be hard to attend his funeral because I did not have $1000 for a plane ticket. My mother did not have the money either. It was very difficult at that moment. I was struggling to travel to Ghana and pay my final tribute to my father, who gave me a chance in the United States of America. But God had a plan for me. I spoke to Douglas about this situation. He told me that Syracuse University's Hendricks Chapel offered financial support to students in such circumstances. He made some calls and gave me the correct contact information of the person to discuss my situation with further.

I went to Hendricks Chapel building to meet the person. I do not recall her name; she was a doyenne with a big lovely heart. She welcomed me warmly to her office and offered her condolences as well. I described my current situation to her; she replied by saying they would purchase a ticket for me to travel to Ghana and bury my father. I was in tears; and could not thank her enough for all her support. She told me to take my time and find a date that worked best for me.

I left her office full of memories of my dad and a feeling of being taken care of. I was used to relying on myself so to receive help when I most needed it gave me a jolt of happiness in a dark time. I never thought something like that was possible. For a university to financially assist me at such a tough time caught me by surprise.

As the semester progressed, I had to make the tough choice on whether to do summer REU or not. This was a very important decision because I was in my junior year and needed to build my resume. I made the decision not to spend my entire summer in Ghana. I wanted to come back as soon as possible to participate in the summer REU. My previous REU with Dr. Ben was a great experience as it paved the way for me to understand how engineering research is conducted.

This time around, I chose to work with a different professor to expand my horizon. My fall semester class with Dr. Glauser allowed me to develop a good relationship with him as I gained more insight into his field of research. He specialized in acoustics and high-speed jets for civil and military applications. Most of his work is defense-related contracts. I went back to him during the spring semester and asked if I could work in his lab during the summer REU.

His research lab is super advanced. The ideal student who is selected needs to have certain classes under his or her belt to understand even a fraction of his work. Our conversation went well. I remember him asking if I had taken all the necessary classes and earned good grades.

I completed the application for 2015 summer REU and he signed it before handing it to my advisor for the final processing. I was very happy to get a chance to work in his lab because only a few students a year get that opportunity. To me, it was a huge accomplishment.

Once I secured this REU for the summer, I went back to the Hendricks Chapel to tell the woman the date I would like to fly out to Ghana. I opted to stay for two weeks because I felt that would be adequate to bury him and mourn his death with my family. These fourteen days will also give me a chance to hang out with my siblings and see some friends from middle school as well. The fall semester ended, and I informed Dr. Glauser about my situation. He was fine with everything.

PART – V

CHAPTER 11

FATHER FUNERAL PREPARATION AND SERVICE

i.   Second Year: Junior Summer 2015

After my semester ended in May, my mother was getting ready to go back to Ghana. I went back to NYC to help her gather all the necessary things. I remember accompanying her and my half-siblings to purchase the suit my father would wear to his grave. It felt like yesterday that we were all having conversations and laughing loudly in our living room. Now I looked up, down, front and back; I couldn't hear his voice anymore. He was gone forever. I don't believe that when someone dies, he or she goes to heaven. However, if I am wrong and heaven does exist, I know one day in my future, he will look down from above and be proud of me. It was very emotional. I informed my mother that, I would join her soon in Ghana. My father's funeral was scheduled toward the end of June. Therefore, she went back to Ghana in May to manage all the necessary preparations for the funeral service.

I prepared to depart for Ghana a few weeks after my mom. I had one big luggage full of clothes that I couldn't fit into anymore. My brother, Clement could wear them. I arrived in Ghana about a week before the service. When I landed in Ghana Accra, my aunt and one of the twin siblings behind me, Mavis, came to meet at Kotoka International Airport. I was very happy to see them; it was the first time in five years. Mavis had grown up beautifully. I remember giving both of them a BIG hug. I arrived late at night. I rested, and the next day we departed in a coach bus to Ashanti Region, Kumasi, where my family is from. When I arrived at the family house, everyone was very happy to see me. I remember one of my grandparents running towards me to give me a big hug. It was a mix of emotions within the family, my nieces, cousins, and the whole extended family.

The funeral service date arrived, open casket so people could say their last goodbye. Before the funeral service in the church, there was a viewing at his family house. He was dressed and adorned like a king, which is an Ashanti tribal custom. He wore Ashanti woven Kente with jewelries all over this body. All the people who came to his funeral service mourned him as they walked past his body in an open room to pay their final tribute. The room had two doors, entrance and exit, to help streamline the procession of mourners.

After a few hours, he was changed back into the suit we had purchased in New York. It was an emotional day for everybody. I remember my mother had to be restrained by my grandfather and some of her sisters every time she walked into the room to see his body because she was in such deep sorrow. I remember all my siblings, including me, went to where she was sitting to offer comfort. All of us were in tears. My father was a well-known man. He had a big heart and always wanted to help others.

Many people attended his funeral service. After a few hours, his casket was closed and ready for conveyance to the church. I was a pallbearer, transporting his casket to a Catholic church and finally to the cemetery. It was very hard. At the grave, I said, "Thank you for all you have done for us and may your soul rest in perfect peace. I will make you proud by taking care of my siblings on your behalf." I picked up some sand and threw it on his casket before they covered the rest with sand after the pastor prayed. That day felt special. Something inside me was very happy, and I wish I could explain, but I cannot. That night, my soul was filled with joy because I was able to come back from America to say a final goodbye to him.

About two days later, I went to see a couple of my friends from middle school and people who knew me growing up in my local town. They were very happy to see me after five years. Some of my friends had moved away from the town. In my eyes, they had all grown up to be big men. I remember them saying exactly the same thing to me. I remember some telling me that my native language dialect had changed when we were all talking and laughing.

My two weeks in Ghana ended, and I flew back to the United States. I remember crying in the airplane when the landing gears lifted off from Ghana soil. I knew that he was in a better place. My mother spent the rest of the summer in Ghana with my siblings.

CHAPTER 12

BACK TO COLLEGE

i.   Second Year: Junior Summer 2015

Whenever I came back to New York City, I prepared myself to go back to Syracuse to continue my research. I went back to the lab and work with the PhD students. It was a fresh start, with many things to catch up on in the laboratory. The work that they were doing was too advanced, and my undergraduate knowledge was not thorough enough for me to play a critical part in the work. The project centered on jet propulsion and noise reduction in advanced aircraft engines. I had to read many research papers to get up to speed on what was happening in the lab. It was a good experience. The knowledge that I gained in the lab made me decided to pursue graduate studies at Syracuse. I knew that with my master's degree, I would get a better job.

There was a minimum GPA requirement in order to be admitted into the graduate program. My previous GPA from last semester was low due to my family situation; this brought my overall cumulative GPA slightly below the minimum target. I had to work harder in my senior year in order to make the cut. It was a huge task, but I stayed positive and believed that I could do it.

Our summer REU program ended and I wrote a summary report based on what I had learned during the program. I also presented my summer project. I was very happy that everything worked out in the end after such a difficult time. I was ready to start my senior year.

ii.   Third Year: Senior Fall 2015

My last year in college! I remembered where I had started and thought of where I was now. I had learned so much and worked so hard. I had to continue the momentum and finish my senior year in a strong way. Before the spring semester ended, my roommate and I had decided to move out of the house. I needed a place for the upcoming fall semester. My friend Joel Rosado had joined his other friends from freshmen year in a five-bedroom apartment. They had one spot left. Joel told me to join them and sign a lease. It was very cheap.

Joel became the president of Syracuse University's Formula One Society of Automotive Engineers (SAE) at the engineering school during his senior year. He is very practical engineer as well as a great personality, which made him an excellent leader for the SAE chapter at Syracuse University. I got a chance to learn more about cars because of him.

Once the semester started, I went back to Douglas and the amazing woman at Hendricks Chapel, thanking them for all they had done for me. It was truly a remarkable moment. For Hendricks Chapel to do what they did to assist me financially to say a final goodbye to my father— that will stick with me for the rest of my life.

This time, all my classes were very interesting, including propulsion, aircraft performance & dynamics, and design & analysis of aerospace structures. I remember my first day on an airplane, flying from Ghana to the United States, I was puzzling how this piece of metal stayed up. Well, the time had finally arrived for me to learn about aircraft engines, maneuvers and the structural design holding this thing together. It fell like a dream come true.

A professor named Dr. Green taught me aircraft performance and dynamics. It was a fascinating class, as I learned about airplane control surfaces, lateral, longitudinal, static and dynamic stabilities, wing aerodynamics and much more. I was showing up at her office hours constantly because I was struggling with the concepts of aircraft control surfaces and their various functionalities. She had a small model of a Cessna 172 (I'm convinced) in her office, and every time I went there, we would use it to go over some of the dynamics of how each control surface helps the pilot to perform certain maneuvers such as roll, yaw pitch, banking, etc.

Dr. Ben also taught me aircraft and spacecraft propulsions systems. It was very cool to learn about different kinds of aircraft and rocket engines as well. I enjoyed all my remaining classes as well. The semester ended, and I was ready to enter my last session as an undergraduate.

Meanwhile, I had talked to Dr. Glauser about the possibility of doing graduate work with him, and he accepted my decision. He urged me to study harder and finish strong with my bachelor's. I took his recommendation to heart as I prepared for the next semester.

iii.   Third Year: Spring 2016 (Senior Year)

I was almost at the finish line. My last semester as an undergrad, I looked back at where the journey started. No role model to guide me, just self-belief, humility, and perseverance had gotten me this far. I knew that I had more work to do as I prepared to enter my next chapter as a graduate student. Nonetheless, I took this opportunity to celebrate as well.

I spoke to Douglas about graduate school. He was very satisfied with my resolution. I informed my mother about my decision. She was a bit concerned because she wanted me to find a job so that I could support her and take care of my siblings back in Ghana. It was a difficult choice for my family, but I assured her that I would do my best to support them while pursuing the two-year degree.

I had two remaining courses as an aerospace engineer, Introduction to Space Flight and Synthesis of Aerospace Systems (our senior design project). The rest of my classes were all electives. I enrolled in courses that could be transferred to my graduate program. This was a smart decision because it would reduce the number of classes that I had to take in graduate school. If I passed these classes, I could complete my master's degree in a year and a half. It was a tough challenge, but I was ready for it.

My senior design project was very special. I was in a group composed of three members including me. The task for each group was to design a radio-controlled Unman Aerial Vehicle (UAV) with the goal of maximizing the flight time on a single battery charge while carrying a pizza box filled with golf balls. It was an interesting project. My team worked tirelessly to complete the project on time. It was grueling, but we were able to utilize all the knowledge that we had gained throughout the four years to deliver this project.

The final flight demonstration was scheduled at the Carrier Dome, sports arena for Syracuse University. Some parents and friends showed up to cheer for some groups. Local Upstate News Network also came to witness this event. It was an incredible and very emotional day for me as well. All the hard work and plenty of sleepless nights had finally paid off. My team was able to fly successfully, and at the end of the event, we were very happy and proud of ourselves. After the event, I was interviewed by the local news to give insight into the project. I expressed what aerospace engineering is about: HARD WORK. My semester ended in a wonderful way; I was admitted to the graduate program to pursue my master's degree.

What were the odds to beat the odds and achieve something of this magnitude as someone from Ghana, West Africa, with no role model? I was overwhelmed as I prepared to graduate with a degree in aerospace engineering, a real *Rocket Scientist*. My family came to Syracuse for the first time to show their support at my graduation from the College of Engineering and Computer Science. It was a long drive for them, their first trip to Syracuse Upstate New York. They left NYC around midnight the day of my graduation. The families of my roommates and other friends got to town (Syracuse) a day or two before our graduation.

I remember when my name was called, and I walked across the stage, they were shouting my name. All my friends did too. After my graduation, we took plenty of pictures. My family was very proud of me. The first person to graduate from college on behalf of my late father, Kwasi Banahene. As I said before, I do not believe that people go to heaven when they die, but if I'm wrong, I know that Kwasi was up there, with a big smile all over his face. It was an emotional day for my family. After graduation was over, we went back to my apartment to have refreshments. They brought plenty of food, Ghanaian food. My roommates got a chance to taste African food for the first time, like jollof rice with baked chicken, which is one of the most famous African foods, especially among Ghanaians and Nigerians in West Africa. They all enjoyed the meal. I remember all my roommates saying,

"Sam, this is delicious."

I kindly replied, "Welcome to my kingdom."

They were all laughing. My family drove back to NYC later in the day. That moment was very special for my family and me.

PART – VI

CHAPTER 13

GRADUATE SCHOOL

i.   Summer 2016

After my undergraduate years, all my friends had left to pursue the next chapters in their lives. I wished all of them best of luck with their future endeavors. Joel accepted a job offer from Ford Motor Company in Michigan, while Teddy got a job offer from Lockheed Martin Sikorsky in Connecticut. Evan got a job offer with the United States Air Force in Washington DC. Breezy graduated a year before me in 2015 and received a job offer from Lockheed Martin in Upstate New York. Anthony Moretti received a full-time job offer from Morgan Stanley in New York City, while Gabriel started to work for his father's business. I was filled with joy as the

134

marvelous people that I came across made it after years of hard work. I was very happy for all of them. It was hard to lose these amazing people, but I had to continue my journey. I did know a few acquaintances from my undergraduate studies who chose to pursue a master's degree.

I had to find a place to live before the fall semester began since my roommates had moved on. Fortunately, Anthony Pegues (Big Tony) had taken a year off and was finishing up in the upcoming school year. We found a place together on Walnut Street. The previous year, he was living on that Street with other two amazing people that I had encountered during my undergraduate studies: David Cabral (Caucasian) and Mohammad Zahid (Middle Eastern). We all used to day-drink sometimes when the weather permits.

I got a chance to know Cabral on a personal level. He shared similar family story as mine and we became brothers from another mother. They both graduated in 2016 and moved on with their future careers. When they moved out, there was vacancy of two-bedroom apartment on the second in the same building. This was closer to campus than all the places I had lived previously. It felt amazing. Therefore, I signed a lease with Big Tony and helped each other move our stuffs to our new place. Without waiting any further time, I was back in Dr. Glauser's research lab working with the PhD students.

This time, my knowledge horizon had expanded, and I was able to make a better contribution compared to my previous summer REU program. Dr. Glauser and the Mechanical and Aerospace Engineering Department covered my tuition. It was a great feeling. The only remaining concern was housing, so I took loans to cover that portion. I was being paid while working in his lab and that was enough to cover my meals. As the semester approached, Dr. Glauser selected me as one of the teaching assistants for his undergraduate class. This was a class that I once took during as an undergraduate in the fall semester 2014: Mechanical and Aerospace Engineering Laboratory. I was nervous and excited at the same time.

My primary role was to provide instruction, grading, lab supervision, and guidance to the students, and report back to Dr. Glauser. The laboratory experiment for this class was divided into four: Solid Mechanics, Signal Processing, Vibration, and Fluid Dynamic. There were four teaching assistants for the course including me. We all worked in the same lab.

Each one of us took the lead in one topic. I selected Vibration because it was one of my favorite subjects during my undergraduate class, taught by Dr. Green. I received money from our department every work for being a teaching assistant. This provided me with additional income. This allowed me to support my mom financially as well to take care of my siblings.

I registered for three classes. Dr. Levy, my man from Brooklyn, taught one of them! I was very excited to have him again as a professor. My fall semester was off to a great start.

ii.   Graduate School: First Year Fall, 2016

Time management is a critical part of graduate school. I had to make sure that I was ready. I wanted to finish my master's in a year and a half as I mentioned before. My classes started well, and I was enjoying my graduate journey. My research work had also slowed down a bit due to the workload during the regular semester. This gave me enough time to study and prepare for my teaching assistant position.

As time passed, I developed a good relationship with most of the undergraduate students. One day I was walking by one of the computer labs at Link Hall (Our engineering building). I saw some of my students, busy at work on their lab report. One said to me, "Sam, we want to be like you and help change the 'hood. I will pursue my master's once I graduate." I took that comment to heart and kindly replied, "You are right; let's keep the hard work rolling." That moment stood out to me. Some minority students were following my footsteps. Not many of us pursue a career in engineering.

During my undergraduate studies, I was the only African American pursuing a career in aerospace engineering. It made me ask myself: Are African American kids not exposed to math and science at an early age; do the school districts not receive enough money to establish an afterschool programs to help develop interest in such a field? Alternatively, is this something most of us (minorities in the United States) do not care about? Would we rather pursue a different career due to the lack of role models? If my second thought was correct, then it was my duty to utilize my platform to become such a role model in the future. I liked thinking about it. It felt good to inspire others.

It was time to register for spring semester classes. I met with Dr. Glauser, and he gave me a recommendation on classes. He was my advisor for graduate school. I signed up for three classes as usual. I couldn't believe that I was almost done with my first semester in graduate school after my long journey. I never thought I would make it this far.

One night my neighbor, David Zuleta, and I decided to go out for a drink before finals at Marshall Street, a few minutes away from my place. David was another minority from Colombia. He is one of the most positive and mentally driven individuals I have ever encountered. David envisioned developing a technology to combat drug overdoses. He was a young entrepreneur on a mission to change the world and make it a better place. I had met David at the gym, Archbold Gymnasium. It was a place for both of us to detox our stresses and recalibrate our brain after a long day at school. We became good friends, and he ended being my neighbor at my new apartment.

On our way back home, we endured a horrific incident. Two Syracuse police officers pulled in closer to us, driving in the wrong direction. They both rushed out of their car and approached us. Without saying anything, one officer pushed me to the hood of his car, spread my legs and started to pat me down. We both asked, "Officer, what is wrong....I'm a student...Sir, I'm a student....I can show you my ID."

They refused to listen or say anything. David was very confused as to why I was being harassed by these two officers. As the harassment continued, two Caucasians, a male and female, got out of the back seat of the officer's car. They were both drunk; the female pointed at David and said, "He is the one that stole my phone." That is when we both realized what was going on. She claimed David was dancing with her at a night club that we had not been to.

David was furious and asked the officers, "If I'm the one being accused of stealing her phone, why is my friend being patted down....because he is black? This is purely racial profiling." As the incident continued, we saw a Syracuse University Department of Public Safety (DPS) officer approaching us. I waved at him, and he stopped. He rolled down his window. The two police officers reversed their car and took off. I wanted to explain to him what had just happened to us. The DPS officer said, "You are too drunk and it's better for you to go home and sleep it off." It was a very tough moment for both of us.

The next day, we went to DPS office to report the incident. We met with the head of that unit, an older Black man. We explained everything to him and his assistant, a white man. They said, "Okay, guys, we will investigate this situation and I will give you guys a call or send out an email later with our findings." The same day, we also went to the Syracuse Police Department (SPD) to file a complaint. Which was the right thing to do as well.

About a week later, we received a letter from SPD that our complaint was under investigation. It was very troubling for a few days given what had been going on nationally in terms of racial profiling by police officers. I used to watch the news about racial profiling incidents on CNN and other channels. So often Black men's lives were taken by white police officers with flimsy excuses. Now a similar thing was happening in my life. It was very hard to swallow. Nevertheless, we stayed positive and walked away with our lives. It could have ended differently, but we handled the situation in a professional manner. The semester ended, and I stayed in Syracuse during the winter break to work at the Carrier Dome.

iii. Graduate School: First Year Spring, 2017

My first semester in graduate school was a great learning experience. The critical component was time management. Working in the research laboratory, grading undergraduate lab reports, preparing for recitations, being available during office hours, answering students' emails, and on top of all of that, my actual three graduate courses for the semester and my racial profiling incident. There is no doubt that time management played an integral part in being able to finish my semester in strength. I continued on this path as I prepared for my upcoming semesters.

As my spring semester approached, I received an email from Dr. Green with an offer to become a teaching assistant for her undergraduate course. A class that, once again, I had taken during my undergraduate studies. I enjoyed her class, Vibrations. I remember class participation being part of our final grade. Therefore, during lectures, our names were randomly called to answer questions. Points were awarded for the correct answer. This made me prepare for her class every single session because you never know when your name would be called. It was a wonderful approach to get students engaged. I registered for three courses, including one with Dr. Ben. My semester was off to a great start.

When school started, I was expecting to hear something from Syracuse University DPS about our racial profiling incident. Unfortunately, that did not happen. On the other hand, we received a letter from the Syracuse Police Department saying that they had investigated the incident and would take internal disciplinary action. Because of school and operating on a strict time schedule, both of us chose not to pursue the case.

It was very troubling especially with our own DPS who failed to send us an email or even a phone call after the detectives claimed they would be investigating the incident.

On the academic side, this semester was crucial. I would be graduating at the end of the 2017 fall semester. I was eager to gain some experience in the industry to boost my resume.

I was applying for summer internships, hoping that I would land one. I applied to many internships, including big and small aerospace companies, but I ended up not receiving any offers or interviews. It did not bother me that much since I knew that Dr. Glauser's research lab offered similar work that was applicable to the aerospace industry.

During the semester, Dr. Glauser received a research grant from the Federal Aviation Administration (FAA) to investigate drones' impact on human contact. This was a great project to be part of as I worked with selected members from my research group. During the drop test demonstration, a local news station, NBC, was present to report our analysis. At the end of our assessment, Dr. Glauser selected another team member and me to interview with Syracuse local news NBC to give a brief overview of our analysis. It was a great honor for us to represent the entire team.

About a week later, we received information that our report had been shared with multiple NBC local news stations across the nation. It was a team effort to make this happen.

My teaching assistant position was also going well. I had the same undergraduate students from the previous semester. Most of them knew me already. They filled my office hours to gain a better understanding of the topics being discussed. I ended the semester with excellence.

Letter from Syracuse Police Department

Frank L. Fowler
Chief of Police

Joseph L. Cecile
First Deputy Chief

DEPARTMENT OF POLICE

Stephanie A. Miner, Mayor

Shawn M. Broton
Deputy Chief

Rebecca E. Thompson
Deputy Chief

14 February 2017

Samuel Banahene
█████ Walnut Avenue
Syracuse, New York 13210

Dear Mr. Banahene:

This letter is to inform you that your complaint has been investigated by the appropriate personnel and a report of their findings and recommendations has been forwarded to me.

You can be assured that I will take the proper administrative action in this case.

Sincerely,

Frank L. Fowler
Chief of Police

FLF/pdh

i.   Graduate School: Summer, 2017

During the spring semester (2017), Dr. Glauser informed me about an upcoming conference in Denver, Colorado, with the American Physical Society (APS) a nonprofit organization. APS is the second-largest association of physicists in the world. Their objectives comprise scientific meetings, research journals, international activities and many more.

This special event was the 70th Annual meeting of the American Physical Society Division of Fluid Dynamics. The event was going to take place in November. He asked if I wanted to author a poster for this meeting with one of my research team members. It was a great feeling to be handed this opportunity. I became the first author of this paper. An abstract was due during the spring semester, and together with my research teammates, we were able to put together our abstract after various feedbacks from Dr. Glauser and other PhD candidates in our research group.

When I first started working in his lab, I saw multiple research posters on the walls from his formal students, who are now succeeding in the industry. I told myself that one day a poster with my name would be hanging on the wall as well. Here I stood, given the opportunity to become the first author for a poster for this upcoming APS conference. It was a dream come true. I worked on this paper with my colleague tirelessly to get it done before the event.

We made a schedule to work around it. Our drafts were viewed during our research meetings and feedback was provided by Dr. Glauser other PhD candidates. Besides this, I continue to engage in my research with the PhD students on advanced jet propulsion projects. Before the end of the summer, I went back home to New York City to spend some time with my mother.

ii.   Graduate School: Second Year Fall, 2017

The semester was full of joy; hard work pays off. Self-belief, perseverance, a hardworking attitude, fantastic personality (humble) and patience have gotten me this far. However, my journey was not yet complete, and I could not get off track. I had plenty of things to take care of, including job hunting. We had an upcoming conference in Denver, Colorado.

Dr. Glauser selected me as a teaching assistant for his undergraduate class again. This time it was a lot easier because I took into account the feedbacks from the previous students to improve my teaching. I was on track to graduate at the end of the semester.

Job-hunting was on top of my list. Knowing the competitiveness of today's engineering market, I tailored my resume to have a chance at landing a job with a top aerospace company like Boeing, General Atomics, Lockheed Martins, Raytheon, United Technologies Corporation, Northrop Grumman or SpaceX, just to mention a few. Not only did I have to polish my resume, but I also had to practice common interview questions and answers as well.

Without having any experience in the industry through summer internships, I was a little worried about getting a job with one of the above companies, but I knew that Dr. Glauser's research lab offered me experience beyond what one might encounter through a summer internship. This gave me confidence moving forward with my job hunting.

I received my first job interview with United Technologies Corporation in Troy, Ohio. I was very excited and nervous at the same time. I did my best to prepare for the interview. The company paid for my flight, hotel, ground transportation and meals. After my interview, about a week later, I received an email from the hiring manager; they were moving forward with other candidates. I was very disappointed, but I took it as part of the learning curve to excel at interviews.

November arrived, and it was time for the APS Conference. I was very excited about this opportunity. Dr. Glauser paid for everything, including flights, hotel, and meals. The conference was great, covering a lot of scientific research from various fields in fluid mechanics and physics. I learned plenty from this conference both academically and professionally. The other attendees who made posters and I presented our work during the poster session.

The event took place during Thanksgiving week; therefore, the university was closed. After the conference, I flew back to Syracuse before heading back to New York City to spend some time with my mother as I prepared for my final semester.

As the semester wound down, the pressure on me increased. I had applied to more than sixty jobs through websites like Indeed, Monster, and various companies' career websites but no luck so far. I remember my research lab colleagues used to ask me, "Sam, any good news?" and I would reply, "Nothing so far." Nevertheless, through all, I stayed positive. I had phone interviews with companies like Boeing Helicopters in Pennsylvania, General Atomics in San Diego, Pratt and Whitney in Connecticut. I also had a phone and in-person interview with SpaceX in California and McGregor, Texas.

SpaceX flew me to McGregor, Texas, their engine development facility, for a position to work on their new Raptor Engine, which will propel humans into deep space in the future. It was very tough as most of these interviews ended without a job offer. I found it difficult to focus on my academic work. However, I knew that patience is the key, which is one of my fundamental principles of success. We all operate on different time schedules, and I had to trust the process but not rush it. God had other plans, and I had to be patient.

The semester approached its final weeks. I presented my capstone project to a select committee, which is a requirement for a master's degree candidate at Syracuse University. It went well. I just had to make minor changes based on the feedback from the committee. My last finals week arrived, and I completed my remaining classes' final exams and projects.

It was a mixed feeling. I had completed my master's degree but had no job offer yet. Fall session poses a challenge in terms of job offers compared to the spring session, which is when most companies open up to recruit new candidates, but I kept pushing. I had a couple of phone interviews lined up, including The Aerospace Corporation in Los Angeles California. An in-person interview with Lockheed Martin Advanced Development Programs (ADP) and their Satellite Division in Palmdale and Sunnyvale, California, for their up-coming Black Engineering Year Awards (BEYA) event in Washington DC. I found out about this event on LinkedIn and registered for it.

Unlike many companies, The Aerospace Corporation is a nonprofit organization that provides technical advice to the United States government on space missions, including NASA as well as commercial customers.

After completing my master's, I had to move out of my apartment and sublet my place. With the help of David Zuleta, who became my roommate after Anthony Pegues graduated the previous semester, I found someone to take over my lease. I sold some part of my stuff like my bed, desk, fan, mini-fridge, office chair etc., to the incoming person to make some money. I moved the rest of my stuff, like TV and clothes, into a storage unit because my mother's place was not big enough to accommodate them. It was very difficult for me.

After years of hard work, I was going back to Westchester, New York, without a job offer. I had to support my mother financially because she was in the processing of bringing my remaining siblings (four) to the United States. It was a difficult time. But something that stuck with me was Rocky Balboa's famous statement about life; *"Life is not about how hard you can hit, but how much you can get hit and still keep moving forward."* My current situation related very well to his famous statement. I had to keep moving forward, knowing that great things were coming my way.

PART – VII

CHAPTER 14

POST GRADUATE 2018

When I moved back to Westchester, it was tough. I had to sleep on the floor with only a few blankets. My siblings were getting ready to come to the States from Ghana. I was wondering where they were going to sleep if I didn't get a job by then, so my mother could afford a new apartment. I saw my stress and pain through her eyes—what every mother feels for her child in tough times. She continued to pray to God every day. She didn't tell me, but I could feel it. It felt like going back in time, but I knew that the future was bright.

One day, I received a call from The Aerospace Corporation in Los Angeles, California, about my phone interview with the hiring manager, Shawn Lin, for a

154

position to work on launch vehicles (rockets) and space vehicles (satellites) for the United States Government. I prepared for the phone interview as usual. However, something was completely different compared to my previous interviews. The hiring manager only asked a few technical questions regarding how suitable I was for the position. I was able to answer all the questions.

He then asked personal questions. This stood out from all the interviews I have had previously. I was very surprised. He was not interested in trying to see whether I was ready to do my job one hundred percent if I was hired. He knew I was coming straight from college with no experience in the industry, especially the available position. He wanted to know if I had the potential to succeed if he hired me. The kind of work that they do, you learn it on the job; universities do not teach this advanced technical material.

He began by asking: "What made you decided to pursue a career in this field?" He then went on to ask about my family. I was very emotional as I began to describe my passion and my journey to my current situation. We went on to have a great conversation after my interview. At the end of our conversation, he informed me that the recruiter would get back to me for the next phase of my interview.

As soon as the call ended, something clicked in my mind and I felt like this was it. It was very strange as I continued to process what just happened during our sensational interview. Meeting a stranger, not even in person but on the phone, and being that open to talk about personal matters! This will forever be something that I cherish about Shawn Lin.

About three days later, the recruiter got back to me with a message from the hiring manager that they would like to bring me in for an in-person interview. We found a date that worked for us. She explained to me the interview processing, the requirements, flight, ground transportation, hotel and meals. She was very polite and thorough with her explanations. I thanked her for all the support she provided. About a week later, I flew to El Segundo in Los Angeles, the company's headquarters, for my interview. I was very nervous but, at the same time, fully prepared. It was a daylong interview.

It started with a one-on-one interview with the project manager (Level III), followed by an interview with the senior engineering specialist, followed by a presentation to selected members including the head of the subdivision (Level IV). My presentation went well, and I answered all the panel's questions. After that, the hiring manager, project manager and one engineering specialist took me to lunch. Once we got back, I had another interview session with the remaining team members. Finally, I completed with the hiring manager as we went over my resume, and I answered a few additional questions he had. The interview was finally over, and he informed me about the next phase. I was exhausted when I got back to the hotel.

I flew back to New York the next day. I arrived very late and got home around midnight. I also had another interview with Lockheed Martin in Washington DC. The next morning, around 5:30 am, I drove from Westchester to DC for my interview. It was a big event with plenty of companies looking to recruit new candidates. I had two sets of interviews, for a position in their Advanced Development Programs (ADP) also known as Skunk Works in Palmdale, California, and their Satellite Division in Sunnyvale, California. The interview went well, and both managers said they would get back to me in a week or two.

A week and half later, I received a call from the recruiter with an offer on behalf of The Aerospace Corporation. She explained the offer letter to me and asked me to choose a start date. I was desperate to start work soon so I told her "in three weeks' time," taking into account the transition period from New York City to Los Angeles.

The company covered all my moving expenses to Los Angeles and even gave me three months in a hotel. These three months were to buy me sufficient time to find a place to live. In addition to this, they assigned me to a relocation agent to help me find a safe and affordable place to live.

Once I hung up the phone, I was in tears as I screamed Yes! Yes! Yes! Yes! Finally! Words could not describe how I felt, knowing that my job search was finally over. I informed my mother, and she gave the glory to God.

Two and a half weeks later, I moved to Los Angeles in March to begin my new chapter as a rocket scientist, where I would be specializing in vibration, shock, and acoustics assessment for rockets and satellites for the United States Government including NASA.

People dream about the California life. The Pacific Ocean breeze, all-around good weather, mountains, plenty of places to explore and experience Mother Nature with Hollywood on the distro as well. WOW, how did I get here? Never did I think that I would be here, but I'm here through Chasing the Unknown. Life is full of surprises, and this job was certainly one of them.

Through this, I am able to assist my family with a new apartment where they feel great and live comfortably. I continue to provide financial support. The journey doesn't end here, but surely, I should take this moment to celebrate with my family and all the people who believed in me, such as my high school counselor, Ms. Williams, my manager, Shawn Lin, friends and finally my late father. If heaven does exist, I know he is up there jubilating, saying, "Kid, you did it."

CHAPER 15

CONCLUSION

My brothers and sisters, what can you learn from my story? I have seen it all: death, racial profiling, poverty, working full time as a high school student, my high school counselor crying in front of me, hustling from the street selling sneakers, plenty of rejections from jobs as a young African. Life could not have been any worse than this, but through all, I stayed positive and stuck to my philosophy. Now here I stand as a rocket scientist and that is what defines the American Dream. My hard work, self-belief, and perseverance had gotten me thus far. I had a vision, a price that I must pay and eyes observing from a distance to see if I would make it in America.

We all have greatness within us, and therefore, "you do not have to be perfect" because "you are just perfect." At the end of the day, it is not about "where you are starting," but rather, "where you are going." Throw that "I am not good enough" attitude away. Step outside your comfort zone, and you will discover the rewards that come with your personal growth. Samuel started with zero, born in Africa, zero role model, made zero excuses, did zero complaining, and set zero limitations for himself as he set out on this journey towards the Unknown; the rest is history.

My roommate David once said, "It's about overcoming adversity and not letting where you come from determine your fate." It is okay to be judged by others but remember this: why should a wolf worry about the opinion of sheep? Be the wolf and do not let the sheep who could not achieve its dreams walk you out of yours.

It is fine if you have to walk your journey alone. Your personality can get you to the finish line. Be generous and kind because kindness is contagious. Learn how to appreciate humanity. Set an example for your family members, friends, and even your nemesis. There are great people out there, such as Douglas, Dr. Glauser, Dr. Green and Dr. Ben; you just have to show them why you deserve their help. Your personality is the key to such an inquiry.

Keep your circle to a minimum; always surround yourself with people you can learn and grow from, even when most of your friends do not understand. It is okay to say "no" sometimes and learn from your mistakes. If Samuel can achieve his dream, so can you. The sky is the limit.

Remember my fundamental bullet points. BELIEF IN YOURSELF, HUMILITY AND PATIENCE. I hope my story will now inspire you to set out on your journey. It's NOW or NEVER; go out there, catch your dreams and achieve your goals. Signing off.

ABOUT THE AUTHOR

Samuel O. Banahene is a professional rocket scientist at The Aerospace Corporation in Los Angeles California. His current work involves shocks, random vibrations and acoustics assessment for Launch and Space Vehicles for the United States Government Space Missions Program.

*****

In this Arena, there is No Talent. Only Hard Work. No Excuses.

Made in the USA
Monee, IL
25 November 2020

49498445R00104